A Life in 16 Films

Born in Coventry and educated at the University of Oxford, Steve Waters has taught in schools, at the Universities of Cambridge and Birmingham and is now Professor of Scriptwriting at the University of East Anglia. He lives in Impington, north of Cambridge.

His many plays include *Limehouse* (2017), *Temple* (2015) (both for the Donmar Warehouse), *Little Platoons* (2011), *The Contingency Plan* (2009) (both for the Bush Theatre), *Fast Labour* (2008) (West Yorkshire Playhouse and Hampstead), and *World Music* (2003/4) (Sheffield Theatres and Donmar). His works for radio include *Miriam and Youssef* (2020) and *Fall of the Shah* (2019) for BBC World Service; *Saving the Blue* (2017), *Deep Swimmer* (2016) and *The Air Gap* (2012) for Radio 4; and *Bretton Woods* (2014) and *Scribblers* (2015) for Radio 3. He has also written *The Secret Life of Plays* (2010), which like his plays is published by Nick Hern Books.

Other works by Steve published by Bloomsbury include *Europa* (2013), co-authored with Lutz Hubner, Malgorzata Sikorska-Miszczuk and Tena Stivicic.

A Life in 16 Films

How Cinema Made a Playwright

Steve Waters

methuen | drama

LONDON • NEW YORK • OXFORD • NEW DELHI • SYDNEY

METHUEN DRAMA
Bloomsbury Publishing Plc
50 Bedford Square, London, WC1B 3DP, UK
1385 Broadway, New York, NY 10018, USA
29 Earlsfort Terrace, Dublin 2, Ireland

BLOOMSBURY, METHUEN DRAMA and the Methuen Drama logo are trademarks
of Bloomsbury Publishing Plc

First published in Great Britain 2021

Cover design: Ben Anslow
Cover image © zimindmitry / iStock / Getty Images Plus

A catalogue record for this book is available from the British Library.

A catalog record for this book is available from the Library of Congress.

ISBN: HB: 978-1-3502-0522-2
             PB: 978-1-3502-0523-9
             ePDF: 978-1-3502-0524-6
             eBook: 978-1-3502-0525-3

Typeset by RefineCatch Limited, Bungay, Suffolk

To find out more about our authors and books visit www.bloomsbury.com
and sign up for our newsletters.

This book is dedicated to my sister Sue Firth
and to the memory of our parents
Yvonne Waters (1941–2016) and
Derek Waters (1939–2018).

Contents

Thanks and Acknowledgements

This book was written in a fury during the first lockdown in 2020 when the only thing getting me out bed in the morning was my family – my son Joe, my daughter Miriam and my wife Hero; they endured the sudden upsurge of memory and the dive into the great canon of film and have been my first guides and critics, enabling fresh judgements on treasured movies. For that ongoing conversation I am deeply grateful, and this book is informed by my love for all of them and as well as the memory of those lost to us in recent years – my own parents and my mother-in-law Doreen Chalmers.

My sister Sue was also a vital collaborator in excavating the memories that inform these pages; likewise my great friend Stephen Meek. The lucid comments of Graham Saunders, Diane Roberts and Chris Megson were instrumental in getting the book ready and without the advocacy of Anna Brewer and Meredith Benson at Bloomsbury I would have fallen at the first hurdle. I am incredibly grateful for the decades of support from my agent Micheline Steinberg, as well as the tolerance and inspiration I get from my colleagues and students at the University of East Anglia – in particular thanks go to Jean McNeil and Rebecca Stott, my vital first readers, and to my scriptwriting comrades, Sian Evans, Ben Musgrave, Molly Naylor and Timberlake Wertenbaker, with whom I have discussed so many of the films in this book.

Writing the book has evoked memories of so many conversations and years of film-going and those who shared those experiences are too numerous to mention here; but Pete Cowley, Richard Curson-Smith, Kathryn Pickford, Ginger Rinkenberger and John Smith all deserve a mention as fellow actual or would-be film-makers, while I remain indebted to my Oxford teachers Valentine Cunningham, Susan Hitch and Thomas Docherty; to Victoria Wohl as film-goer and interlocutor; to David Edgar as my mentor, Terry Johnson as my first director and the much-missed Sarah Kane and Clare McIntyre; to Sarah Barrow, Matthew Carr, John Hopkins, Helen Nicholson, Peter Raby, Karen Reader, Jane Stanley, Steve Watts, David Whitley and Jean Welsh as fellow Cambridge cineastes; to Gemma Bodinetz, Ben Jancovich, Jenny Topper for their early faith in me; to Marc Beeby (*i.m.*), Sebastian Bourne, Paul Bourne, Jack Bradley, Ian Brown, Nathan Curry, Howard Davies (*i.m.*), Polly Findlay, Michael Grandage, Rob Hastie, Tamara Harvey, Chris Haydon, Nick Hern, Caroline Jester, Mike Longhurst, Patrick Morris, Jeremy Mortimer, Gbolahan Obesisan, Josie Rourke, Clare Slater, Caroline Steinbeis, Boz Temple-Morris, Chelsea Walker, and all the other talented artists and actors who have supported me on the writing journey.

Preface: *Dark Waters* – The Last Movie?

I defied the injunctions for one day only.

I had a feeling that the experience of going to the cinema was about to vanish as the pandemic advanced. Poorly cleaned cinemas with recycled air seemed perfectly designed for coronavirus incubation as strangers spluttered through boxes of popcorn, spraying microbes hither and yon – was any film worth the risk?

Frankly these days all too few. Only a year earlier I had angrily refused to renew my Arts Picturehouse Card at their feeble programming: vanishingly few subtitled films and those screened corralled into inaccessible daytime slots. The adrenaline rush of the film bucket list was diminishing steadily, weeks passing without any spur to mount the bike and head into town. Cancelling my membership was prompted, paradoxically, by my attending a newly restored print of Nicolas Roeg's *Don't Look Now* (1973), screened at the bizarre hour of 12 p.m. I wasn't prepared for how seeing this film again would affect me. Moving indoors from a warm June day into the sterile darkness to see a film I thought I knew off by heart felt a perverse sort of pleasure. A guilty pleasure!

After the plethora of car ads and drinks ads and deodorant ads and ads for films that barely sustained interest for the duration of the trailer, after the tautologous self-promotion of the very cinema chain I was patronising, finally – finally! – it began.

'Don't Look Now'.

In a film about second sight, you hear the action first.

Roeg like his coeval Robert Altman sets sound against image. We *see* the dank abyss of a pond in a deep English garden interrupted by the trawl of a reflected bright blood-red mac but we *hear* the painfully slow piecing out of a simple piano melody. A child mutters a song, the piano plays ponderously, another child's bike sheers through ice and then a rogue mirror; indoors Donald Sutherland squints over a slide of the interior of a Venetian church, Julie Christie leafs through photographs.

Silently the girl in the red mac tries to rescue her red ball from the dank pond.

A strange electronic curlicue! Sutherland startles, a shaggy-haired boy runs into the house, sound gives way to the primeval groan of a cello as the father takes a deep husky pained breath and wades into the lake where his daughter has soundlessly sunk, in a Cubist tumble of broken images. He doles out mouth to mouth, sliding about on a muddy mound, in a desperately real scrabbling.

Back indoors, Christie wanders to the window to glimpse her globe-eyed husband bearing their dead daughter like some sodden Lear ('howl, howl') – her scream fuses with the sudden shrieeeeek of a drill.

FX: Monotonous clangour of Venetian bells; pigeons erupt from a wintry square.

We have begun.

Exiting from the rapt viewing of a film I've watched on and off since I was 12 (on late-night television, on VHS, in classrooms with students) I felt a sudden stab of grief at the slow death of this, for me, the pre-eminent art form. Where are such films now, once astonishing mass audiences, now reduced to a niche experience in the middle of the working day?

The cinema's schedules declare what is lost: more screen time devoted to ponderous tours round art galleries, airless streaming of boulevard plays, tedious operas at the Met, or back-to-back multiplex hits and franchise fodder.

Full of furious intimations of film's demise, I blurted to the bewildered woman at the till that, no, I will not renew my membership card and as I walked out, suffused with cheap triumph, blinking into the June day, this book flashed into my thoughts. How I would write my life defined by the films I had seen, the films that had shaped me. How I would write a love letter to a dying art form.

And I calmed down and got on with life.

A year passed; and then as Covid-19 advanced across the planet like a bedside mourner I went to see a film one last time. Frankly any film. What's on?

Dark Waters. Dir: Todd Haynes. Starring Mark Ruffalo.

This modest American movie reminds us of how cinema, as critic Siegfried Kracauer observed, seeks to redeem the world through, '*recording and revealing physical reality*'; or as André Bazin, another great film thinker added, '*every film is a social document*'; or as his protégé, director Jean-Luc Godard noted, every film, even a work of fiction, is a documentary of the actors acting. For a film is not just a window onto the world, it is a *piece* of the world, preserved. At the start of his great work *Theory of Film* (1960) Kracauer recalls that after watching his first movie he jotted down the title, '*Film as the Discovery of the Meaning of Everyday Life*'. That could serve as the subtitle of this book.

And in preserving reality, a film reveals its many facets:

It is a commodity, shaped by an industrial context.
It is a form of technology mediated by the tools with which it is made.
It is a literary document, a work of narrative, shaped with words.
It is a work of design, with nothing left to chance.
It is a series of performances preserved for posterity.
It is a landscape.
It is music.

It is sociology, geography, anthropology and politics all at once.

It is art.

It is life.

Dark Waters.

Immediately I am seduced by Ruffalo's crumpled Brando features, squashed into ordinariness as he mimics an environmental lawyer taking on chemical giant DuPont. Note his tic of stress, this Theseus in a maze of a dusty backroom filled with boxes of tedious documents. His uninflected performance metes out the procedural pleasure of film that tracks a hidden reality.

Ruffalo: I first saw him in Kenneth Lonergan's *You Can Count on Me* (2000); how he's aged! I remember a beautiful young man, part of a tradition of American acting of high mimetic seriousness, graduate of the Stella Adler academy, and, like so many film-makers I love, possessing a stage pedigree. *Dark Waters* rehashes the same numb moral questioning that lit up his Oscar-nominated performance in *Spotlight* (2015).

Ruffalo dials it right down. His performance is massy and slow and he seems to grow fat in front of us, resisting glamour even as his face retains its ghost. He's also a producer here, and I suspect is the reason this film even came to exist – and my God, he looks good driving ugly, nondescript cars; and how well he listens, soaking up the moral weight of the circumstances, while clearly trying not to turn the movie into a hagiography of the lawyer he's impersonating.

Ruffalo reminds us that in film the actor is no mere character, they embody and exemplify the film's ethic. His slow, shy manner mirrors the film's slow, stoical reveals. He's slightly humourless yet allows the odd fleeting smile to uncrease his steadfast frown; in a time where men are seen through a lens of suspicion, he disarms through moral stealth.

But this is cinema so we attend to the quality of the light as much as any performance. Ruffalo's Mount Rushmore head is sculpted in Ed Lachmann's grainy images, announcing an affinity with four decades of independent cinema, not least Haynes's own oeuvre – *Far From Heaven* (2002), *Carol* (2015) – spiralling further back to the high tide of critical independent American cinema, the 1970s, when cinema began for me. Who could watch Haynes's film without seeing at the same time Alan J. Pakula's comparable '*paranoid trilogy*': *Klute* (1971),*The Parallax View* (1974), *All the President's Men* (1976)? Surely Lachman's grey palette signals an intertextual lineage with Gordon Willis's chiaroscuro work for Pakula (and Coppola), just as the tendency for the camera to drift away from the given subject is an allusion to the slippery deep focus zoom that peppers Rossellini's late work or all of Antonioni. This minor film doffs its cap to its ancestors while training its gaze on a contemporary crime.

I am a playwright. I should respond first and foremost to the screenplay, but I have to confess so often it's the camera's work that grips me, the '*camera-stylo*' as Alexandre Astruc characterised it in 1948, '*writing ideas*' in its own idiom, here clarifying the world's injustice. Would a chemical corporation in plain sight manufacture Teflon, a product with which they knowingly poisoned their clients? Yes, the camera asserts, yes this happened. But it says so in its own language, transcending mundane dialogue and banal scenes; for only in film can the facts of how we are situated in the physical world – let's call them phenomenological facts – be truly explored.

Film is always about figures in a landscape and it presents them with a forensic distance it's perpetually attempting to bridge. It shows us a world of deeds – driving a car, leafing through ring-binders, pained typing, demolishing a meal, opening a beer, shooting a cow – transactions with the world as much as transactions with people. It's fascinating to watch Ruffalo pore over the software of the late 90s, or decoding obscure chemical formulae. And we watch cinema together, yet alone; and because we are together, the room hums with alertness; but the film solicits us as individuals, as opposed to the theatre where we are in constant emotional contact with those around us. And perhaps that's why films are so often concerned with loneliness, privacy and voyeurism.

And while film is in dialogue with itself as much as with the wider world, it brings us the world all the same, demanding we look closely in conditions of rapt attention, conditions that arise from its being projected in darkened rooms among others. *Dark Waters* seems to cry out for television: it has a socially concerned TV movie theme and trades in conventional tropes of family. Yet in contrast to TV it offers an emotional descent into the work of finding the truth, an epistemological journey as much as a narrative one. Look, it seems to say, and look again; note the weird behaviour of that cow, the unfeigned rage of that Virginian farmer; connect the swanky big pharma reception with the child born with one nostril. This then is an event – making this film, watching this film, turning capital to good effect.

A film worth risking in a time of pandemic.

I was among an audience of maybe fifty souls with whom I felt a sort of foolish solidarity. I flinched when anyone sat near me and left by the side stairs. Everyone seemed old; the habit of contemplative watching akin to church-going is surely dying. I left wondering when – and if – I would be back.

And also wondering how this all began, this passion for film-going; and why it seems to matter so deeply to me and to those I am close to. And wondering about the ways I have been *formed* by cinema, how I've grown up within it, intellectually, emotionally; how the very commitment to something called 'film', to something so often derogated as 'art-house' has taken shape in me even as I have worked in a parallel medium I care with equal passion for, theatre. Is my position in one medium looking over lovingly into another tenable? Is it possible to love both forms equally?

Kafka claimed he '*had no literary interests but was made of literature*'; have I likewise somehow been made out of film? As the philosopher Stanley Cavell remarked in his work on cinema *The World Viewed* (1971), '*memories of movies are strand over strand with memories of my life*'; I too have been formed from those '*hours and days of awe*' spent in the dark of the cinema.

So I began to track how my experience and experience of cinema became intertwined. Where and how did it start? For it's not simply a question of films viewed but also of the cinemas and the cities of those viewings. Experiences of film have entered my life in a given place at a given time and informed that moment. There is a geography to my viewing just as there is a politics and a history to it; a *cineaste* is made not born.

But there's a larger question behind this exploration, a political question even. With much of the world labouring under right-wing regimes, as we negotiate the double jeopardy of climate crisis and pandemic, film's eclipse seems symptomatic. I was born at the tail end of the baby boom, into a world within which this mass art form aimed at gathered publics was still flourishing. This world was also one of white privilege, profoundly patriarchal in its workings, and films too often reflected that. For much of my life I have watched films written and directed by white men, only belatedly becoming mindful of the sheer oddity of that. Ironically this hegemony is ending just as film cedes its primacy as an art form to streamed television dramas available on the world's many devices. For all that these dramas emulate film, too often they lack its experimental and existential reach.

Let us be clear – there are more than sixteen films in this book but those that guide each chapter represent turnings points in my life. They are not all great films; some I actively dislike. Some may be pedestrian in form but so significant in their moment that they survive their limitations. They are not the films I ought to like either, revealing my impeccable taste or unimpeachable political credentials; you can't re-edit your life like you can a film, splicing in the films you now wish you'd seen. But they define moments in time and space and track the progress of my life and the lives of those close to me.

I am under no delusion that my life is any more interesting than any other, but it's the only one I know well enough to speak of how film shapes all our lives. But I *can* be seen as a representative of an era, as someone born in the relatively stable time of what historian Eric Hobsbawm described as '*the Golden Age*' of social democracy and coming to adulthood as it was steadily dismantled into the neoliberal landscape we now find ourselves in. My focus is England, a small nation on the edge of a continent it imagines itself distinct from, with a denuded tradition of film-making caught between the industrial output of America and the parallel tradition of continental Europe. The travails of film-going, making and criticism in this country run in tandem here with the political trajectory of the last fifty years, the long descent from Harold Wilson to Boris Johnson, from the welfare state to a nation 'left behind', from prosperity to austerity, from decolonisation to Brexit. This is the story of my family and my nation as much as me.

Act One Becoming

1 *The Wizard of Oz*: Primal Screen

(COVENTRY)

I was born in the final third of the century of cinema.

For my parents, Derek Waters and Yvonne Best, movie-going or, '*going to the pictures*' as they called it, was a habit only beginning to wane as television began to assert itself. By the moon landing we had a black-and-white set in our Cheylesmore home on the edge of the city of Coventry where they'd moved in 1961. A hastily married young working-class couple, they were economic migrants from Portsmouth, drawn to the industrial hotspot of the Midlands where manufacturing in general, and of aeroplanes in particular, sucked in labour from across the world.

They'd wooed each other in Portsmouth jazz clubs, dance halls and flea-pit cinemas where dad and his Teddy-boy pals would boo on-screen kissing, but where they edged closer to each other in the warm smoky companionable fug of double bills, buying treats in the intermission, all priced to their pay packet. Cavell, growing up in wartime and post-war America, noted that for him '*movie-going was casual*'; my parents, likewise, would go night after night, week after week, breathing in films as casually as we browse the Internet.

Dad liked westerns and thrillers, mum liked comedy, musicals and '*women's pictures*', anything with a '*good plot*'. For dad, Hollywood had established America as the epitome of modern masculinity in its egalitarian storytelling; for mum, it offered glamour, colour and escape – and she had plenty to escape from. They lapped up all things American: American jazz not British rip-offs, American rock 'n' roll or soul not British knock-offs, and always American movies.

This went deep, right into the basis of who they were. Mum claimed that her very name, Yvonne, with its exotic provenance, was inspired by Canadian dancer, actor and singer Yvonne de Carlo; a fact somehow linked to her elusive heritage. Her mother Molly (whose actual name was Helen, which she disavowed) was married to Jack, a merchant seaman and former miner from Newcastle-under-Lyme who'd come south in the Depression. But in contrast to mum's three other siblings, Jack cared little for Yvonne, perhaps because her birth in 1941 sat uneasily with his tours of duty.

She passed her eleven-plus but was prevented from going to grammar school because the uniform was too expensive; school ended at 15. As soon as she could, she fled her cramped terraced home in central Portsmouth to work in hotels where she would learn to fend off predatory male guests. Then she got a job in a Hawker

Siddeley engineering plant, displayed in a booth at the entrance like the female clerk in Henry James's *In the Cage* (1898), punching time cards as the men flowed in; one of them my dad.

What made her happy? Moped rides with girlfriends; espresso bars; her ferociously guarded freedom. One refuge was in nearby Southampton where her Aunty Doris lived in a house overrun with cats, every surface covered with pages of unfinished romantic novels gathering fluff on chairs, sideboards, behind cushions. Doris spent her pension on cream cakes and sherry. In that cave of working-class bohemia, mum's disputed origins made sense. Nonetheless, the question remained: where had her exotic name come from?

De Carlo, only emerged in the movies at the precise point mum entered the world adorning numerous film noirs such as *This Gun for Hire* (1942), a version of Graham Greene's novel, in which her only lines are *'Cigarette, sir?'*, and moving up the credits until her breakthrough in *Salome, Where She Danced* (1944). Her striking dark features resembled my mother's own black beehive, kohl-flecked eyes, 'sulky' unsmiling yet puckish looks in contrast to dad's lanky, needy, confused masculinity.

For him, movie narratives of violence spoke to the great struggles of his time he'd missed out on. Born just after war began in November 1939, he grew up on the outskirts of Portsmouth in Cowplain. One of his first memories was the astonishing sight of Canadian and American troops marshalling outside his window as D-Day approached, which sat uneasily with the fact that his father Cecil (who disavowed his given name Cyril as unmanly) didn't serve himself, thanks to an eye injury acquired as a boxer. In a further irony, dad came of age just as National Service ended. His sense of missing out on *'doing his bit'* and proving himself, informed his taste for American films and the glut of movies euphemising war in the 1950s and was further reinforced by the imperialist yarns he devoured in comics like *The Eagle* or the Biggles novels of Captain W. E. Johns. School was a chore and he constantly found himself in the headmaster's office for cheek, finally walking out at 15. His destiny like many of his class was skilled manual labour.

So for both parents adulthood began early. Within three years they'd met and married.

Their wedding photo stares down at me now, a family group assembled against the rear wall of a municipal hall. Dad's dark hair is thick and side-parted, mouth open in a gap-toothed smile, tie touchingly askew; mum's dazzling in veil, high cheekbones, dark brows raised as if in surprise, her own mum Molly in a vampish fur coat, waspish curved glasses, next to dad's mum Kit, guileless, handbag on sleeve, cake-shaped hat. Jack's raised up on a patch of grass, marginal, amiable grin, as if relieved to have his first daughter off his hands. Cecil's lost at the rear, retreating behind thick-rimmed specs and toothbrush tache, his habitual deafness leaving him at one remove. Dad's brother Brian is not in shot – perhaps he's behind the camera; mum's sisters Lena and Frances look gawky and shy, barely resembling their older sister.

So they move to Coventry, ostensibly for higher wages, actually to escape – for mum, from the oppressive mystery of a household where she was the object of daily belittlement by Jack, now an alcoholic doorman at the Queens Hotel on 'Pompey seafront'. For dad, from the kindly but emasculating world of his respectable working-class home, Cecil housebound, Kit paralysed by anxiety (she once burst into tears of shock at his sprinting down the shingle into the sea at nearby Havant).

Somehow they reconciled what they wanted from the pictures although for years mum lamented dad's preference for 'war, war, boring old war'. Robbed of her deserved Oscar for *Little Women* (2019) Greta Gerwig observed that 'male violence' still determines cinematic seriousness; and I note how now, with both parents gone, I struggle to recall mum's predilections in film-going against dad's clearly asserted ones. He'd sabotage any film she selected which he considered unworthy with a barrage of sighing and fidgeting and she would respond in kind with a live full-voiced renarration of the plot, refusing as she put it to be 'ssshhed'.

Coventry, with its large, young and diverse population, was well served with cinemas, most of them now bingo halls. I remember two. The first, on Far Gosford Street was the Paris, adorned by a neon Eiffel Tower, intimate and invoking Sacré Coeur in its odd onion dome and was walking distance from us, near dad's works. The other was the Godiva, a vast barn on the Earlsdon Road where gas-guzzling cars produced in that very city pulled up to discharge viewers; for like the America revered in the cinemas, Coventry was a city built for and around cars.

The Godiva boasted the capacity to project in CinemaScope and its vast charmless structure embodied where cinemas were headed, the multiplex and the mall – huge rooms of darkness soon to be subdivided into more intimate screens but for then designed to accommodate thousands. This dark egalitarian space asked no questions of you; an usherette with a torch ripped your ticket and smuggled you into your row.

Here films played back to back in double bills and you could get lost for an entire day, entering at midpoint for one, seeing the next entire, leaving when you reached your point of entry. People were forever edging their way in flickering light along endless rows of irritable fellow viewers. Beneath the seats a landfill's worth of discarded paper cups, popcorn tubs, shed lolly sticks and burned-out fags accumulated. Yes, this was cinema as Americana; out of town, bulk-based and industrial. The building, like a story supermarket, told no story itself. As Larkin noted of the 'Large Cool Store', it was, 'synthetic, new / And natureless in ecstasies'.

The Paris offer something rather different – a whiff of glamour, a sense of the wider world, speaking to the city's global reach. Coventry, far from exotic, nonetheless had a kind of bitter fame thanks to the saturation bombing the city endured in November 1940, leaving 554 dead and the centre a heap of rubble. It was an icon as much as a place, its identity forged through total war.

The destruction of St Michael's Church by incendiary bombs, rendering its nave roofless, framed by smoke-darkened sandstone gothic tracery, elevated the city into a symbol of the sorrows of war; indeed, made the city cinematic. After all it had featured in stirring Pathé footage. But the city itself provided extraordinary 'haptic *shocks'* in the idiom of Walter Benjamin, montage effects of scorched stumps of medieval buildings framed by bleak flyovers and underpasses, modernist architecture a jump-cut away from the Gothic. Basil Spence's magnificent new cathedral embodied this – built adjacent to the ruins, it was a jewel house of modernist art by Graham Sutherland or Jacob Epstein, and had only just been inaugurated in 1962 graced with the debut of Britten's shattering *War Requiem*, which internalised cinematic editing into its musical form, with modernist and sacred music jostling for prominence.

We were twinned with other wounded cities, Volgograd, Dresden, or Belgrade, the latter providing the name of our theatre built with Yugoslavian timber in 1958, itself a gesture of defiant socialist art where the great early plays of Arnold Wesker or Shelagh Delaney had their debut. Then there was the innovative central shopping precinct borne out of architect Donald Gibson's visionary pre-war design; as the most unapologetically modern city centre in the country, it resembled post-war Eastern Europe as much as provincial England.

As you shopped there you might notice memorials to other destructions; for instance, Lidice Place, its plaque marking the massacre in that village in Czechoslovakia, 1942, perpetrated by the Nazis in reprisal for the assassination of Reinhard Heydrich (the subject of Brecht's only successful screenplay in America, *Hangmen Also Die* (1943), which Fritz Lang wrangled away from him, as well as inspiration for visionary British film-maker Humphrey Jennings's *The Silent Village* (1943) transposing the same events to a remote Welsh community).

Yes, Coventry through its trauma had become a world city; and the glamour of the Paris Cinema seemed in step with that, as it was with the city's growing population of workers from South Asia and the Caribbean, Poland and Ukraine, all converging on the city's factories, and who we lived alongside as neighbours.

I wasn't permitted entry into the Paris which rarely showed 'family films' but I would fixate on the laminated glossy 'coming attraction' stills pinned behind glass screens, piecing together the contents of the 'A' and 'AA' and 'X'-rated movies shown there. Like Antoine Doinel in Truffaut's *Les Quatre Cents Coups* (1959) who filches black-and-white stills of Harriet Anderson in Bergman's seminal *Summer with Monika* (1953), I'd drool over the filmic possibilities these images presented, windows onto an illicit reality.

I'm haunted to this day by stills for two films forever confused in my mind, both subject to the interdiction of my father. They were both revisionist American westerns, films that we'd later connect through (such as Robert Benton's *Bad Company* (1972), which introduced a fresh-faced Jeff Bridges to the world; or Dick Richards's *The Culpepper Cattle Company* (1972)), a vein of work unleashing a strand of American self-scrutiny in the wake of the Vietnam War. The first, *Soldier Blue* (1970), pitched hyperbolically as '*the most savage film in history!*' was an incendiary dramatising of the 'Sand Creek massacre' of the Cheyenne and the Arapaho peoples by the US Calvary, echoing atrocities by US forces in Vietnam, such as My Lai. Those striking images of navy blue uniforms set against harsh Colorado landscapes melded with a very different re-envisioning of American colonial history, *Little Big Man*, also released the year I turned 5, directed by the great Arthur Penn and featuring Dustin Hoffman, fresh from *The Graduate* (1967) and startlingly theatrical as Cheyenne progeny and buddy of Wild Bill Hickock.

I pleaded with dad to let me see these *adult* films with a yearning so deep it seemed bottomless – the injustice of it! The arbitrariness of the British Board of Film Classification! The titles were childlike in their force; 'blue' was the word my parents used to describe some piece of inappropriate comedy or banter; 'Little Big Man' sounded fun and child-like, where would be the harm in that? What hurt me further was dad, who never uttered an untruth if he could avoid it, refused to denounce the films outright – oh yes, he'd seen both films and valued both films. He'd even bought Dee Brown's 1970 history of the genocide of Native Americans, *Bury My Heart at Wounded Knee* on the strength of them, provoking a rethink about the founding of America and the ethics of war informing the notion of what he would call '*gratuitous violence*'. Yet while I learned these debates were not for me, I also learned that same violence and sex defined that adult kingdom of cinema.

So the Paris was for me a site of the adventure of film, of adulthood, of the distant, of the foreign. Whereas the Godiva, named after Coventry's legendary nudist (who rode out hourly from a clock on Broadgate, her nakedness obscured by long tresses) provided my cinematic primal scene.

For it was in the Godiva that I have my first real image of being in a cinema and for all of us this is, to harness outworn Lacanian language, the true '*stade du miroir*', a place where private reverie collides with public being. But worse, this was the site of my first film trauma.

It happened during a double bill so upsetting I've repressed the second half of it – I know one of the movies was *The Wizard of Oz* (1939), forever haunted by the horror of that hot afternoon in a thinly attended screening with mum and my sister Sue. What was that other one? Was it the equally nightmarish *Scrooge* (1970)? If so I hated it as much as I hated Oz.

We forget how frightening film is. I know my mum did, who doubtless thought this was a way of killing a long summer afternoon stuck with a 4- and 6-year-old. What was this shapeless building, the raked auditorium, the massive screen where the Panavision images of Ronald Neame's or Victor Fleming's films would occupy my entire perceptual reach? The big screen indeed, a haunted palace, filled with darkness and unlocatable sound. We entered mid-film, into a strange mixture of dark and light, a hushed passage into a womb with a view. '*Shh, shh, Steven*' – my hand gripped too tight, my sister annoyed at my thrashing around, her clumsy, often wordless brother, denizen of a special school in nearby Sherbourne Fields, bedevilled with extreme dyspraxia, and always, always deeply embarrassing. I was the sibling who had pulled focus again and again, with my incapacity to sit up and hold myself erect, cunningly posed for 'normal' family shots, yet profoundly challenged in coordination, language acquisition, literally speechless until I was 4 years old.

And up there on the screen, the sheer overwhelming creepiness of an old film veering from hard-etched black and white (that terrifying tornado, a whole house caught in its vortices) to garish, hyper-vivid Technicolor. The coercive charm of it, the sickening green of the Wicked Witch, feet protruding out from under the weight of the house that flattens her like a bug. The horror, the horror!

But what terrified and fascinated me in equal measure was that sound. Huge speakers posted at all corners rip any utterance from the actors and hurl it into dark space; amplified whispers, shouts, screams. And the hatefully loud music, brassy and shrill, manipulative and searing. In my dark seat, too little for my small body, designed to tip me back into the dark, I felt my fear convert into something more familiar, the warm trickle of piss down my leg. I didn't tell mum as I knew she would be furious, that I would certainly be hit, as any child in 1970 would be if they soaked a worn-away velour cinema seat with their own urine. But eventually the smell gave me away and her embarrassed fury was electric!

I am grabbed, dragged along the row, stepping on toes and tripping on coats and bags – shh, shh, a hydraulic hissing – I become the spectacle, not the film. I have disrupted the public dream and I will be punished in the harsh glare of the smelly loos.

Needless to say, I've not hastened back to either film. I first took my son aged about 5, too, to see the late Pixar movie *Cars* (2006) and I remember his face, those dilated pupils, the turmoil within him between wanting to stay and wanting to leave the nightmarish sublime of darkness, massive image, bone-shaking music and sound design, and most of all emotion – emotion pictures! In his suspended state of awe and terror I saw my own fear back then.

The child at the cinema reminds us of the totalitarian force of moving pictures, of this tool of mass agitation, delivering as Susan Sontag said of Leni Riefenstahl's films '*fascinating fascism*'. Film is the vulgar *Gesamtkunstwerk* Wagner craved, the audience in Stygian darkness, the action illuminated onstage, the orchestra sunk in the pit, a '*mystic gulf*' between the drama and the viewer. In even the dullest film everything is pitched to an operatic intensity. How timid television seems in contrast, tuned to the everyday; how tame films are when they are rescreened there, emasculated by cropped image and tinny sound. The dream of Panavision in which *Scrooge* was filmed or StereoScope or the much-vaunted 'Sensurround' linger in the pointless excitement of 3D or Imax, which pummel the audience into submission through sheer immersion, fearing any break in attention, any drift, any loss of connection. For film is deeply vulnerable to the sudden opening of the fire escape doors obliterating the screen with natural light, revealing its vampiric nature.

So my entry into film was not auspicious – but between the Paris and the Godiva, just as on the streets of this impossible jigsaw of a city, torn between adult critical sophistication of the Paris and the normative abyss of the Godiva, between the law of the father and the mother, one thing I knew was film mattered.

(LONG LAWFORD)

EXT. A MIDLAND VILLAGE, 1970S. MORNING.
  A BOY (8) in cub scout uniform pulls back a gate
to a large colonnaded house. He hovers on the brink
of the gravel drive. Through large bay-windows a
woman's frame can be seen.
  He crunches up to the door, reaches on tip-toe
for the bell.
  Through frosted glass a figure looms.
  The door opens. We see MRS GRAVES, tall, elegant,
reeking of loneliness, (60s).

            BOY
            Bob-a-job?

EXT. A GRAVEYARD. MORNING.
  A gravestone covered in lichen and moss. A
scrubbing brush sheers across it.
  Pull back to see the BOY on his knees, shorts on,
cold hands scouring A MAN'S NAME from the headstone
under the vigilance of MRS GRAVES.

1971. We move. We move precisely 12 miles along the A428 to a village just outside
the market town of Rugby, Long Lawford. Not far in distance, but we leave behind
modernity for an earlier version of England; and in the process acquire a different
sense of who we are, where we belong.

And what we watch.

Beyond the village edge lay the grounds of Holbrooke Hall, a long gravel
drive, dark yews and tall cedars, inaccessible and turned away from the village which
had grown from it. Old Warwickshire families such as the Boughtons and the
Caldecotts lived secluded lives there, rumours attending on them of poisonings,
unquiet ghosts immured in bottles, intimations of an undead English past worthy of
M. R. James. Lawford, essentially three lanes and an attached council estate and
recreation ground, tapered in its north-west corner to Chapel Lane at the entry to the
estate, where a small Victorian church turned away in sadness from what had

eventuated. Here I performed the bidding of my terrifying neighbour, the aptly named Mrs Graves.

Lawford's an unremarkable place of low-lying arable farmland, between the meanders of the River Avon, the bricked-in dank of the Oxford Canal and the West Coast mainline which, in a fateful moment for the village, didn't grant it a station stop. A place where farmers, sunk in neglect, pre-EEC subsidy, grubbed out hedgerows, binding up the land in barbed wire and electric fences.

One such farm, two streets away from us, run by a Mr Badger, was an untidy sprawl of shitty mud where cows moaned away their lives in stalls among a dismal tangle of ploughs, harrows, disassembled tractors all permeated by the sweet stench of silage. You'd see him periodically, cloth pants tied at the waist with twine, badger-like face compressed in frown. A mile further north lived the Tonnicliffes, a pale Grant Wood-like brother and sister, glimpsed at high windows in their Georgian farmhouse at the Mill, their boundary fence a hecatomb of eviscerated voles and moles pecked at by crows, '*pour encourager les autres*'.

I made friends with Robert, son of tenant farmers on the wrong side of the A428. Their cheery chaotic home was a bolthole, straw drifting in shafts of golden light as we feasted on teas of unpasteurised cream in brandy snaps. I'd help them with their work, following the baler in the wake of its hot noise as it spewed out warm bundles of hay we'd stack and heap and jump off. Each summer a Traveller community descended unbidden on their land at night, an encampment of long caravans and fat cars in the home field. The men shinned up onto the barn rooves, hammering down zinc panels through the long summer day, whistling and shouting to each other. At night they lit bonfires, drank and sang indifferent to propriety, fire filling their faces with shadow and flame light; '*a quiet, pilfering, unprotected race*' as John Clare has it in 'The Gypsy Camp'.

Robert, his two put-upon sisters and me took it upon ourselves to 'defend' the farm. One hectic night we fled a gang of dangerous-looking older boys, heart in mouth, switchbacking through the darkening fields. I holed up in a hedge gap with my secret weapon, a blue goose egg, heavy and surprisingly large in my hand. One of our pursuers crested the broken fence, backlit, breathing hard, close to. Instinctively I hurled the egg at the approaching shadow: smash! The heaviness was gone from my hand; the boy stood, stunned, face glazed, picking fragments of shell from the slick of it, as astonished at my deed as I was having perpetrated it. Neither of us knew what to do next. He walked away. I felt his shame and mine too.

Coventry was a world away. As was the cinema.

But our move coincided with a social advancement; dad, having started on the shop floor of Rolls Royce was promoted to works foreman – as he sang (to the tune of the Red Flag), '*the working class can kiss my arse / I've got the Foreman's job at last*'. His elevation was a mixed blessing as his (newly nationalised) 'lame duck' company found itself embroiled in wildcat strikes, placing him at odds with his former comrades. From time to time I saw him in the massive machine shop, a panorama of men, lathes and noise; he proudly brought home an immaculately fashioned turbine blade, like some Iron Age adze, matte and cool in the hand.

Mum pieced together her portfolio life, moving between delivering car batteries to supporting people who were then called 'the mentally handicapped' in an 'Adult Training Centre' outside Rugby, inspired by the incapacities of her own son, me. Here I met again the community of the neuro-diverse, caught in ecstasies of utterance under the calm gaze of mum and her colleagues, a guileless world of ungovernable feeling from which I had now been removed.

Sue and I didn't always fit into the plan; for our long summer holidays we were dispatched to stay with our aunty outside Portsmouth or my granny who now divorced Jack and became a kitchen maid on a small estate in West Stoke House, a Georgian manor at the foot of the South Downs where we spent our days among the staff watching chickens get their necks broken or wandering into the misty beech woods of Kingsley Vale. Molly, Granny Best to us, like her daughter, was not demonstrative, rarely smiling, cuttingly sarcastic; we were often in the wrong, too loud, too demanding. Now alone after years with her soak of a husband, Granny Best simply wanted to play her darts and have her gin; we were a burden to her.

West Stoke kept us in a pre-war Britain of feudal relations, literally living downstairs in the under-floor-level kitchen where at the peremptory tingle of a bell Molly would shoot off to wait upon the aristocratic householders. One Christmas we found ourselves in a scene from Renoir's 1939 masterpiece La Règle du Jeu, enlisted in the local shoot, as beaters driving hapless pheasants out of the bracken to die in an explosion of feathers for the diversion of the country set, guns broken over their arms, voices braying through freezing fog. Dad sat in wordless humiliated fury at a long bench in the barn among the 'servants' eating our allotted portion of the catch.

Back in Lawford I joined my sister in mainstream education at Long Lawford County Combined, a one-storey spread of temporary buildings at the edge of a council estate. The headteacher, Mr Griffiths, like most of my subsequent teachers from Wales, was a sombre man with a silver crest of Brylcreemed hair. He received me and my sobbing sister with great solemnity, walking us to our classrooms, our hot hands in his large dry palms. I recall him later in a state of rapture at the edge of the hall when the school was deep in song, eyes brimming with tears.

It was a benign enough place, even progressive in its adoption of a strangely laissez-faire approach to early years learning, which from memory was dubbed 'integration', inspired by the Plowden Report of 1967, later famously derided for its turn to 'child-centred learning'. Here was where I began to realise writing was a kind of power. For in practice 'integrated learning' felt like being allowed to spend time writing stories at my own speed in my own way, along with walking into the countryside to study 'landscape history' or engaging in 'country dancing'. We sat on the herringbone-patterned floor in the light-filled hall as a teacher peeled back the wooden panels from a huge television screen to reveal the excitement of a minute's countdown to whatever improving matter awaited us; but my head was full of wild imaginings.

My stories were a confused pulpy affair. 'The Jungle Hut' for instance, riddled with racism and accounts of heavy sweats and exotica; or 'The Amazing Dreams of George Gotobed' labelled by my teacher as 'silly'. Or the 'breakthrough' piece 'Pain', naturally a science fiction work about a space at the edge of the known universe where all pain was produced. But they poured out with little bidding.

Break times were less benign. Thanks to my uncoordinated gait I was called *'spaz'* or my new soubriquet *'Wally'*, which I took for a term of praise. But we had been propelled back into the rough justice of *'the Squirearchy'*, an England of rural labour and intraclass conflict. The kids came from one large council estate and then 2 miles up the road Lawford Heath, an even grimmer estate where defaulting tenants were sent to rot, their children unwelcome to Mr Griffiths who lobbied us to refuse their admittance.

If you got a drubbing in the playground you'd get little sympathy from the smoked-filled staff room. 'Child-centred' here tended to feel like 'child-governed'. To conjure up that heady and often heedless time I need only watch Ken Loach's *Kes* (1969) again or dip into Barry Hines's original novel which moved me deeply years later, from the opening gambit of *'hands off cocks, on socks'* from Billy Casper's thuggish brother Jud, to the final image of Billy weeping for his dead falcon in a cinema: *'Big picture. Billy as hero. Big Billy on screen. Kes on his arm. Big Kes'*. Loach's film captures the scary music of school corridors, bawling burly teachers such as Brian Glover and Colin Welland, sometimes well-meaning, largely uncomprehending; a world of clips round the ear and kicks in the balls – or the 'nuts' as we'd have said.

But unlike my secondary school my primary school steered clear of corporal punishment.

The teachers were idealistic, unrecognisable sorts to me. Take Mr Foster, new in my first year, young, thin as a stick insect, all angles, tall, taut coil of curls on his head, flared suit, driven by some Leavisite imperative to evangelise us with learning. He angrily drew our attention to famine in Bangladesh one assembly in a state of deep political rage, his face flushed as he recalled someone mispronounce it as 'Bangledesh'. And he hurt me deeply by dismissing one of my more florid poems as 'Patience Strong'-like while praising a girl from the estate for having compared a storm at sea to the motions of a *'washing machine'*, a metaphor I considered if I'd known the word, bathetic. The sense of writing as a form of competition was probably established here, with *Schadenfreude* never far away; but I had internalised inflated registers of writing he rightly called out, from sources I wasn't even conscious of – I mean who *was* Patience Strong?

I got more support, albeit mischievously, from Miss Close; another skinny, sardonic figure whose breath had the tang of iron from her breaktime fag. She was delighted when I wrote 'The Great Escape', a brutal satire on all the teaching staff and dinner ladies at the school, egging me on to go from class to class to read it aloud, only to find myself on the wrong end of Mr Griffiths's fury that his team was being traduced by a cocky 9-year-old. If the outcome was calamitous, here was the first intimation of the public power of words. I walked blushing with pride armed with my A4 sides, up and down the school, performing my takedown: look at me, doing the voices, gaining the laughter of friends and foe. Look at me! No wonder in Mr Griffiths's last report, he characterised me as having been 'cock of the walk' in the school. Stories granted me power.

My teachers were mysterious to me in their middle-class leftism. They puzzled my parents too – I felt deep embarrassment when a local brass band played a concert and I glanced round to see my teachers doubled up with contemptuous laughter, mimicking the trombone player. Dad was incensed. Irony was not on.

Our street, Main Street, was largely Victorian, and our house was an old bakery wedged between pubs; on Main Street alone, there were five of them, not including the rowdy British Legion working men's club. The denizens of Long Lawford liked their drink; the village was dominated by several large and often violent households. Top of the pecking order were a dynasty of builders, presided over by its patriarch Keith, a wiry, whiplash short man, face lit up by fag end, in a perpetual scowl, later to become Mayor of Rugby. Indeed during our time he wangled a visit for the schoolkids to the town hall where we gazed into the well of the aldermen's plush raked seats; at the podium he rounded on the current mayor, 'We know you lot think Lawford folk are a bunch of turnip-bashers.'

Dad and mum threw themselves into their new community. Mum ran the Brownies, requiring me to attend all-female camping expeditions, alongside my own hated tenure with the Cubs where two ex-servicemen maintained discipline with a knotted rope and as the only middle-class kid I was automatically made sixer and exempt from punishment. We went on long marches to a campsite in nearby Lutterworth erecting rotting canvas tents, watching the wilder lads leap over fires or threatening each other with sheath knives. I tried to imagine I was in a western; but what role should I play? I wasn't 'hard' that was for sure; I was chubby and crap at knots and I basically wanted to be on my own, 'head stuck in a book' as mum would say.

Dad had discovered walking. He walked the Pennine Way, the Lyke Wake Walk, the South Downs Way, the Coast to Coast Walk; the sight of him in a wet cape disappearing into some peatbog was a common occurrence. Our Sundays were spent waiting for him to get the correct compass reading to decode wet Ordnance Survey maps. He became chairman of the Rugby Ramblers, a breezy community of men and women in kagouls and woolly hats, tapping out pipes on their boots and doling out Kendal mint cake, mild-manneredly reclaiming the land that Marion Shoard in The Theft of the Countryside (1980) revealed had been stolen from us. In this and other roles dad found himself constantly at loggerheads with the village – blocking planning permission for the extension of the Club, complaining about noise, parking and drunken behaviour at our neighbour The Caldecott Arms, bewailing the state of public footpaths, tearing down electric fences in the teeth of splenetic farmers. None of this was designed to make us well-liked.

We'd be startled awake by the thud of bodies against our outside wall as drunken fights broke out in the night; one afternoon two men walked calmly into our sitting room and sat pertly on our sofa, awaiting their pint as if we were the pub. One of my much-hated domestic tasks was to clean the brass on our front door with Brasso to the contempt of half-cut blokes slewing up in Granada Ghias to an afternoon lock-in.

This adversarial state took a toll on my parents' already tempestuous marriage, far from any support networks. My dad tried to maintain good relations with our publican neighbours who characterised him as '*under the thumb*'; one particularly ugly night, Marjorie the landlady appeared at our door with a tray bearing a pint as if to sharpen the shame of dad '*not being allowed out*' to drink himself stupid. As dad accepted it, smiling ingratiatingly, mum slapped it out of his hand; beer splattered over our walls, glass shattered on our porch – what follows is a blur, but I remember her screams as dad, splenetic with piqued masculine rage, chased her up our narrow stairs, Sue and I throwing ourselves between them. I tried to joke them out of their rages and stand-offs, watching mum's face to detect her moods. I learned all I needed to know about conflict at home.

The village considered my sister and I as oddities, not helped by my physical differences. I walked in an uncoordinated and penguin-like fashion, I dropped balls, I was big and ungainly, I even unhelpfully acquired 'man breasts' very early on. I had to define myself through fighting, something I was hardly equipped to do, although granted a degree of height at least. Much of the conflict was tribal; our school was populated by kids from the neighbouring more genteel village of Church Lawford, and so the 'Churchies' felt themselves set against the 'Longies'; out of sheer perversity I sided with the former. To compound our isolation further, dad, a Labour Party member, canvassed for them in this Tory enclave. I tagged along, as we knocked up shabby houses in the former airmen's homes on the Heath, flinching at dogs and receiving dusty answers. Dad backed Bill Price, son of a miner and journalist on the *Coventry Evening Telegraph*.

I fell in with families of farmers living in pre-modern conditions: my friend David who always smelled of piss, his large family packed in a council house in the middle of nowhere; my friend John, crammed with obese parents in a caravan outside the family bungalow where his granny lived alone. John's family's right to graduate into the relative luxury of that bungalow was conditional on his passing the eleven-plus exam. Sadly, he failed.

Yes, this was deep England, the remnant world of George Eliot, red-brick farmhouse fastnesses next to the ash-blighted outskirts of the Rugby Portland cement plant which employed the villagers who found work, its chimney dominating the skyline, pumping out carcinogens, presiding over the shock of a vast quarry; no wonder Tolkien resonated for me – here was the very scoured Shire he wrote of.

But it was also for me a place of freewheeling through carless lanes, picking mushrooms in copses, falling with my Chopper bike into the floodwaters of the River Avon in an unknowing homage to Maggie Tulliver, swirled away in filthy brown floodwaters, squeaking home in weed-filled shoes. The tribalness of it, the sense of '*weird England*' informed my viewing – horror for the world I was in, sci-fi for the one that I hoped for.

My reading, listening and viewing fused. I was a latchkey kid, home when my folks were at work, cleaning the ashes out of the grate, scoffing a crumpet with marmite watching *Clapperboard* or *Screen Test* on the telly. Now less frequently at cinemas, my passion was fuelled by spin-off publications and comics. *2000AD*, launched by IPC in 1977, catered to this hunger, with the thrilling strips of Judge Dredd offering a pleasingly authoritarian cyborg cop in homage to Clint Eastwood's quasi-fascist *Dirty Harry* (1971). More shameless were knock-off complements to pulpy popular cinema – after *Jaws* (1975) came 'Hookjaw'; after the grim slog of James Caan grimacing through *Rollerball* (1975) and *Deathrace 2000* that same year came 'Spinball'. The lurid glamour of the non-certified violence permitted me access to splatterfests my foes the BBFC, or the BBC with their watershed, withheld.

Maybe I was up for dystopia because I was living in one: Britain in the late 70s, collapsing under its own contradictions, even if a more equal nation than it had ever been. The Second Cold War. Terrorist bombs in nearby Birmingham. Blackouts and power cuts. Expelled from Coventry's brutalist modernity into feudal Warwickshire I craved stories navigating that time-slip. I was stunned by the trailer for John Boorman's 1974 flop *Zardoz*, which mirrored the emotional landscape I was in: why else would Sean Connery pony-tailed in skimpy ball-hugging onesy, pursued by stone heads over Irish mires seem so exciting to me?

I needed some sort of salving myth, a substitute religion. I had no formal faith to fall back on. Aged 10 I announced I would be a Methodist and took myself off to services in the local shed-like chapel, much to my family's amused indifference. The young stammering minister queasily received a sudden influx of young kids lured in by the promise of prizes. But Methodism, an unceremonial affair, in no way requited my longings for ecstasy (although I was rewarded for with a box set of the Narnia books). My next station of the cross was to demand a belated christening aged 11 in the teeth of further family incomprehension, declaring my Christian name would be 'Lawrence'; I'd just been ravished by David Lean's *Lawrence of Arabia* (1962), dazzled by Peter O'Toole's sapphire eyes.

While these passions were short-lived, they were symptomatic. I wanted the world to be full of mystery, to be re-enchanted; I wanted to make sense of the bleak freedoms of my new life.

These longings crystallised in an infatuation with Michael Anderson's 1976 film (trailed as '*the first movie of the 23rd century*') *Logan's Run*. Despite Roger Ebert's view of the film as a '*vast, silly extravaganza*' I still get a shudder of excitement at the sight of its flat-nosed hero, the improbably posh Michael York, smirking through the quasi-orgiastic 'Love Shop' scene with scantily-clad Jenny Agutter (from *The Railway Children* (1970) through to Roeg's *Walkabout* (1971) Agutter haunted my puberty). York's character Logan is described in David Zelag Goodman's script as '*strong, virile (yet sensitive) with a kind of austere grace*'. His side-parted glossy blonde hair, plastic spread-out features, thick meaty RP voice all combined to forge an unlikely role model. With his trademark bemused smile, York epitomised the mid-70s transatlantic turn in film-making, blending Hollywood allure with English class: the director was British, as were the two leads, and the evasive patriarch they discover, a T. S. Eliot-quoting Peter Ustinov; who else but that avatar of sophistication could embody *'the last man alive in Washington D.C.'*?

The film's source was a novel by William F. Nolan which I read and reread, its spangly graphics arising out of a domed world criss-crossed by 'maze-cars', a city catering to every desire, but which killed you off at 30 to manage population growth. The hermetically sealed dome (*'a marvellous crystalline city of great openness'*) was self-regulating and severed from the natural – so much so that when Agutter's Jessica finally steps outside to confront the actual sun, she exclaims, *'Is there something on fire?'* This Platonic cave outside history and ecology is a common trope of the time; here the *Planet of the Apes* (1968) Ozymandias moment of Charlton Heston confronting the Statue of Liberty enveloped by the dunes is transmuted into York happening upon the Lincoln memorial covered in liannas, Lincoln's venerable features provoking his outburst, *'I've never seen anyone so old!'*. Like Connery in *Zardoz* Logan is the hero as dupe, a so-called Sandman dutifully liquidating any citizen rash enough to try to escape their allotted span in the ritualised executions of the 'Carousel'. Yet under Jessica's influence he realises this communal sacrifice is a deadly scam, thereby echoing other conspiracy theory narratives such as George Lucas's debut *THX 1138* (1971) or even *Chinatown* (1973), or even back to the archetypal *Wizard of Oz*. Beyond the boundaries of the controlled environment lies revelation in a feral post-human world. The 70's dominant note of scepticism complicates any simple heroism; *Logan's Run* despite its upbeat ending is a drama of disenchantment and a response to population growth anxieties expressed by ecological Cassandras such as Paul Ehrlich.

Yet its domed idyll, shot in a mall in Dallas, is in retrospect simply the Bluewater shopping centre a decade ahead of its opening, a banal steel and glass world of escalators and water-features, an indoor version of Coventry's precinct, its consumerist welfarism already beginning to look tarnished. The flight from utopia mirrored our regression into atavistic England, Logan's journey beyond the citadel mapped onto the scrubby edgelands of our village.

And my parents were changing accordingly, building an extension, seeking self-sufficiency, brewing beer and baking bread, wearing fishermen's smocks and smoking cigars. This process reached its summation one day when I was awoken to the stirring clamour of Shostakovich's Leningrad Symphony playing loudly on their brand-new record deck, vibrating the woofers and tweeters in Twin-Tower-like speakers. They were reaching for a past in a dark present, albeit one idealised without class struggle, a version of the pastoral in a corner of rural neglect.

As a consequence the other genre that spoke to my condition was horror, reflecting the social inertia of our new life. Again, this passion was fuelled by reading, in this case lurid paperback anthologies of shocking schlock edited by the indefatigable Herbert van Thal. I can still see the cover of the nineteenth volume now, plastered with hook lines (*'her brains spattered on to his hand'*), a fat grub oozing from a skull with dislodged eyeball. Individual authors have faded from memory, leaving only a trace sense of sex and dismemberment, prurient and sadistic all at once.

As puberty seized me, horror furnished me with vengeful tales of reaction and misogyny. One evening as dad drove me home from another wild night at the Cubs, I coldly dismissed my fellow cubs as '*scum*'. Dad stopped the car. We sat in silence; the engine ticked and cooled. Then he turned with a fierceness I didn't recognise. He reminded me who I was, who we all were, where we had come from; it wounded me and rightly so. I cried with a shame which I felt all too often in my childhood. I wanted to be right! I wanted to be special! Was I the force of evil or the defender of the good?

Of course I couldn't get into horror films as yet, the BBFC had seen to that, branding them 'X'-certificated; but I could stay up late, gorging on the airless Hammer Horror reruns on the telly, especially those featuring Ingrid Pitt ('*if you dare taste the deadly passion of the blood nymphs*' as the advert for *The Vampire Lovers* proclaims; well, I sort of did dare).

Hammer films, hardly distinguishable from each other, are like masturbatory scenarios, played out in a studio pornographic half-light, a flatly lit vision of post-war England. Their heroes are archly aristocratic and etiolated (Peter Cushing), their objects of fear figures of insinuatingly foreign lineage (Christopher Leigh). This was a perpetually day-for-night indoor world, febrile, bloody and yet coy. In the inaccessible realm of cinema, less crummy low-budget thrills and frights were coming into view, films I could only dream of viewing: *The Exorcist* (1973) provoking moral panic through its realism and excess; or *The Omen* (1976), a big-budget, A-list-cast glossy nightmare with Gregory Peck, the embodiment of American gravitas, dragged into its squalid melodrama of the resurgent Antichrist.

Our local cinema was now the Granada in Rugby which, having opened as the Plaza in the 30s, was on the ropes, floundering to find work that might break the hold of colour TV now boasting three channels. Its final gambit was to screen the atrocious disaster movie *The Towering Inferno* in 1976, a genre rounding up every available star to all go down with the ship or in this case, burn in a high tower, and all-too symptomatic of the sclerotic state of mainstream cinema by the mid 70s. It failed to save the Granada.

I only remember seeing two films there; the first, the pitiful last outing of the 'Carry On' franchise, *Carry on Dick* (1974) which I forced dad to take me to for my ninth birthday. The afternoon proved bitterly drab for both of us, as we watched this mirthless rehash of the highwayman era peppered with tired jokes like 'The Old Cock Inn', or Sid James smirking away as Richard 'Big Dick' Turpin. The other film I forget, but it was with mum, and provided my second cinema trauma as an insouciant mullet-haired guy amused himself by tapping fag ash on my leg during the film. Mum confronted him, which made him and his leering mates square up to us on the cinema steps with a penknife – astonishingly, on a fine day in Rugby, passers-by blithely passed by.

Dismal time, dismal films.

The hope I had perceived in the late 60s, the glamour that film, cinema and life seemed to promise, reduced to long afternoons with my only proper pal Alan, rifling through his brother's 'girly mag' collection, boring ourselves stupid with Uriah Heep albums and faked up seances with Ouija boards in his dad's shed.

Life really had to get better than this.

Then I took the exam that changed everything – the eleven-plus.

(RUGBY)

If anyone were to make a film about the town of Rugby, what would be the establishing shot?

INT/EXT. A TRAIN MOVING AT HIGH SPEED. MORNING.
   A glimpse of the marshalling yards and the endless island platforms of Rugby Station, c.1868.

   Or?

EXT. DRONE SHOT. NIGHT.
   WE swoop over the eerie forest of 800-foot radio masts, their pink lights winking.

   More likely it would start with:

EXT. RUGBY SCHOOL PLAYING FIELDS, 1823. DAY.
   Thumping chords of BEETHOVEN as we strafe the playing fields. A YOUNG WILLIAM WEBB ELLIS idly picks up a football to his fellow players' horror -

. . . thereby inventing a sport which plagues me for the next five years, and causes my dad, a passionate player, to come home weekly with a black eye and another missing tooth.

But why is Rugby uncinematic? What is this quality of the 'cinematic' which Modesto, California, setting of George Lucas's seminal coming-of-age reverie *American Graffiti* (1973) reeks of, or which renders the obscure Bohemian backwater of Lodenice in Jiri Menzil's *Closely Observed Trains* (1966) so riveting? Provinciality is surely not in itself a deal-breaker. Menzil's film is a wickedly funny tracking of boredom under the tyranny of German occupation that subjects its setting to comically detached scrutiny; Lucas lovingly lingers over the lost idyll of his American adolescence. Why doesn't my hometown offer that possibility?

Rugby's typicality is its undoing. Life is elsewhere. Not just a small town but as an estate agent might note, it's a 'market town', with toponyms like Sheep Street indicating its farming roots; its employers latterly engineering firms (GEC, AEI); its USP, transport links – the railways, the M1. Rugby is blandly bang in the middle, neither north nor south, nor, really, the West Midlands. Oh, there's a clock tower where Mods and 'Numanoids' (followers of Gary Numan, that cut-price Bowie) would spar; there are various Victorian buildings, stolid and speaking of nowhere as such. And yes, there's that school, rendering the town an adjunct, its students wandering the streets in fawn blazers touting exaggerated RP drawls.

Well I didn't go to Rugby School, even if I did go to school in Rugby.

In 1977, the year I passed the eleven-plus, I was allotted my place at grammar school, dispensing with my peer group at one fell swoop. For in Rugby then, and maybe now, the map of social exclusion was made graphically clear at age 12. Three out of forty in Long Lawford County Combined passed. Two of us boys went to Lawrence Sheriff Grammar, fawningly named after the founder of Rugby School; one girl to our sister school Rugby High School for Girls. The rest were packed off to secondary moderns, where they would learn, as Elvis Costello sang in his eponymous song, to be 'second place in the human race'.

Surely this shouldn't have happened by the late 70s? When Alan Bennett's *The History Boys* was first staged in 2004, its 1980s Leeds grammar school setting was declared anachronistic by critics. Well, a whole life can be anachronistic and Lawrence Sheriff or 'Sheriff' as we knew it was certainly that. Single sex; staffed by men in midlife or older, those '*belligerent ghouls*' Morrissey sang of, the school itself was a hodgepodge of breeze block and red brick, its main hall rather unimaginatively called 'Big School', its echoing stairwells, rank sulphurous science labs with cabinets of foul-smelling chemicals and of course its rugby pitch.

By 1977 with Shirley Williams education minister, the process of rolling out comprehensives as designed by Richard Crosland, and facilitated by one Margaret Thatcher, had reached its apogee; but in Rugby, the selective system remained in place, with comprehensivisation bitterly contested at the local level. So on went my dark uniform with its crest of our school symbol, the Griffin (celebrated in our school song, '*As long as the Griffin has wings, boys, as long as the Griffin has wings*'), a magnet for disappointed bullies from those other schools I would now not attend. In honour of my new middle-class life my parents bought me a briefcase; unwrapping it on Christmas Day I blushed with rage at what its fake leather represented, hotly refusing to use it. It sat pristine in the utility room, until Dad quietly took possession of it. Yes, that briefcase was a portent, along with the ungainly blazer and scratchy tie; the days of shorts and class mingling were over.

So with my sister heading off to Dunsmore, a rather less antiquated grammar, we'd board the 85 bus for town.

That journey can be my establishing shot for Rugby; the rasp of matches on frost-flowered filthy windows, the air blue with illicit cigarette smoke, initially seated up the back with my former peers, then joining my sister at the front to their contempt; the floor wet with gob and our rucksacks adorned with logos for Led Zep or Yes.

As we crawl up Lawford Road I felt my dread deepening. For all of the ungoverned chaos of my primary school it felt like a realm of light, freedom, and most of all, of girls. Piling off the bus, smelling like I'd smoked ten packs of Benson & Hedges, shouldering my bag, I hear the bell tolling as I enter the school, in the shadow of pitched roof and pseudo-Gothic turrets, traipsing through the archway where the dead from both wars were memorialised, nodding at the obligatory poem by Sir Henry Newbolt, alluding to conflicts that felt on-going in the minds and bodies of our teachers. Then into the dark chamber of Big School where up on the dais masters in gowns sat like dreadful corvids, we boys in ranks according to age in front of them, trying not to catch the eye of older shaggy-haired lads who'd mark you out for torment later.

My first head teacher was an unpredictable white-haired man who would appear without fanfare in our lessons, moving too fast for his years, quick to deploy another anachronism, the cane. We were still eight years away from the banning of what was euphemistically called 'corporal punishment' but here it flourished in a wealth of forms. Perhaps a sharp-edged board rubber lobbed in a fit of rage; maybe a swipe round the back of the head by a passing master; and the ultimate sanction, the stiff phallic cane. I received it once, and in a way rightly so, for a crime that mystifies me now, but which seemed quite natural in that context, having terrorised another boy, slashing his blazer with razor blades. Razor blades! And I wasn't expelled!

We sang tuneless hymns and intoned empty collects ('the Collect for Old Laurentians' for instance). We were divided into houses with meaningless names – Caldecott, Tait, Wheeler, Simpson. And we came together from our very different worlds; outlying villages such as Wolston or Brandon or posh suburbs. The kids from Rugby or Bilton or Dunchurch knew they were a cut above us lot, lumped together in a class that marked our common origins. Indeed, at the end of our first year, we could take the charmingly named 'Common Entrance' exam to Rugby which creamed off the poshest and brightest of us. We spent our days administering a never-ending stock exchange of status, exacted in irony, sarcasm and scorn. One lad, a chubby Yorkshire kid with a froth of wiry hair and a sweet nature, was so relentlessly mocked that after a year he left us for the secondary modern down the road; a decision beyond our comprehension.

The masters were an ill-assorted squad of men, a good proportion of whom were Welsh – Mr Redd the most acerbic of them. Here rugby was no mere pastime, it was a religion and a way of filtering and categorising us. For years, as a well-built teenager, my face a mask of acne, I was under continuous pressure to join the school rugby team, a passport to privilege and exemptions. And for one happy season I was indeed elevated to second row, the so-called 'boiler-house'. Dad was elated; he ran up and down the touchline yelling, 'go on Steeeve', the only parent apparent. Having been harried by Mr Redd for my undone top button and fat tie, the day I made the team these misdemeanours were overlooked.

The game had its cinematic apotheosis in Lindsay Anderson's frenetic film *This Sporting Life* (1963) adapted by former rugby league player David Storey from his own novel and charged with testosterone and violence and launching Anderson's life-long masochistic crush on its alpha male star Richard Harris. But for me those 90 minutes on the pitch were an imposture. Locked in the scrum, some other fucker's shoulder blade in my face, toying at the ball, was my chance to relax and lean in. I made the faintest of waves at the lozenge in the line-out. Most of the time I kept out of the way and out of harm, and with not a single notable achievement to my name, after a season I was summarily dropped.

But there was no respite from our trudge down Lower Hillmorton Road every Wednesday afternoon to the icebox of the changing rooms, chafed legs orange in the cold. I'd found myself catching the attention of a psychopathic bully, one of two wedge-headed brothers; the elder, Michael, bore down on me like a renegade from *Lord of the Flies*, his outsized head in a 30s cut, his face a caustic leer. In an act of frenzied fear, I grabbed his waist in a high tackle, swinging him so violently he brained himself on the metal hooks where our uniforms hung. The changing room fell into an awful silence; well, there was no blood, even as he reeled, got up and attempted to summon up some dignity. Something was understood. But I didn't like what I was becoming.

Years later when we studied Dickens I recognised echoes of the pupil-teacher system in our prefect system, where an elect of older boys lorded it over their juniors with the full licence of the school. This was our lower-middle-class version of the 'fagging' in our mother institution down the road, indelibly captured in *Tom Brown's Schooldays* (1857) and sadistically reanimated in the 1971 BBC TV adaptation, dominated by the terrifying figure of Flashman. Certainly, it enabled gangs of prefects to carry out their own 'Sus' policies, confiscating whatever they cared to, using their privileges to undertake bullying with impunity. I'm proud to say that I was one of only three people never elected to this office in my year group, having been deemed too 'silly'.

The secret of survival was patronage and my new best friend was my ally. Paul was from a council house in Wolston; we maintained one of those teenage friendships which swing between affection and contempt – for him largely the latter. He had the advantage of having a big brother in the fifth form who also had a crush on my sister and therefore looked out for us. Paul and I bonded over cultural matters, getting lost in the woozy refuges of progressive rock (another anachronism in the age of punk; but then the Midlands was the home of hard rock and heavy metal). Foremost here were Genesis and Yes, whose gatefold sleeves couched in cryptic Roger Dean designs provided a kind of kabbalah, Peter Gabriel's wry satire speaking to our condition. We considered 'Supper's Ready' from Genesis's *Foxtrot* a flat-out masterpiece and could quote it verbatim, all 23 minutes of it and together we made the pilgrimage to the newly opened National Exhibition Centre near Birmingham in 1978 to queue for six hours to see Queen live ('*No time for looosers for We are the Champions . . . of the Wooorld*').

Paul also had the sort of dad who had a porn cache, which was another bonus; and Paul was a marathon masturbator, proudly documenting his acrobatic bouts in a manner worthy of Philip Roth. He was an education in other ways; as Labour slid into catastrophic defeat in 1979, he and his family, unlike mine, were insouciant. Jim Callaghan, a Portsmouth man, was a leader they revered, and Bill Price was turfed out in favour of Tory Jim Pawsey, whose son Adrian was in our year (his other son,

Mark, also from Sheriff, would later represent Rugby in David Cameron's coalition government, a notably vocal critic of gay marriage). In Paul's house, no Labourite shibboleths existed; he could deliver a mean imitation of Tony Benn, and his family agreed Margaret Thatcher could hardly do a worse job than the clapped-out Labour government. Paul's dad's liberality extended to taking him to 'X'-rated films. I'd breached the 'AA' line when my Dad took me to the Paris to see *The Outlaw Josey Wales* (1976) stunned by its bleak realism, its repositioning of Eastwood from the horse operas of Sergio Leone to something more autumnal. It was the last western I would see for years and maybe the last film Dad and I truly agreed on. I nagged him rotten to take me to see *Alien* in 1979, accessing my first 'X'-rated film four years ahead of the designated age.

But Paul put such transgressions into the shade; I'll never forget his excitement coming to school hotfoot from seeing Nicolas Roeg's dark erotic thriller *Bad Timing* (1980), a blend of necrophilia, scopophilia and Cold War Vienna, with Art Garfunkel as puzzled as its distributor Rank who denounced it as '*a sick film made by sick people for sick people*', double-billed with Scorsese's urban nightmare *Taxi Driver* (1976), Paul gleefully rehearsing the final revenge fest ('*de Niro has this mad Mohican and he walks into the brothel and shoots this guy in the face and then takes out another and his brains splatter on the wall and and and. . .*') If only my dad was Paul's dad! Admittedly Dad did take me to see Scorsese's *Raging Bull* in 1980, but then boxing was in his blood whereas for me it was tedious and opaque, even while I was knocked out by the monochrome force of Michael Chapman's images – and it would take years for me to understand the closed-off cold appeal of de Niro.

Somehow we managed to sneak into *Carrie* (1976), awesomely tasteless in its fusion of menstruation and telekinesis. How we relished the bullies' cry to Carrie of '*Plug it up! Plug it up!*' cathartically alluding to that utter mystery to any teenage boy, the workings of a sanitary towel! How we loved Sissy Spacek's plain disc of a face streaked with blood! Horror, excess, violence! These interests reached a kind of climax with the excitement of *The Shining* in 1980, Kubrick's lofty overhaul of King's gothic melodrama, a steely fable of isolation and terror, '*serenely frightening*' as David Thomson has it, and an induction into Jack Nicholson, Eastwood's darker rival as male lead. Nicholson's sardonic, countercultural cache opened up the possibility of an ethic of irony and moral ambivalence; his persona, expressed so powerfully in Bob Rafelson's *Five Easy Pieces* (1970), morphed between a hedonistic blue-collar hustler and a self-hating refusenik of his bourgeois origins, epitomised the in-between state of class identity I was negotiating. As Jack Torrance, the blocked writer in the Overlook Hotel, his struggle between passive aggression and something more satyr-like was manifest in Kubrick's characteristic overhead shot, bearing down on his forehead and receding hairline, eyebrows with upward satanic flick, predatory eyes and carnivorous grin, a cornered animal.

But in general now the Granada was closed, Rugby had little to offer in the way of film. From time to time the Benn Memorial Hall had screenings; I took myself there aged 12 to see creepy soft-focus French soft-core movie *Emmanuelle* (1975). It was there that I first saw *Mad Max* (1979) as noisy and unedifying as the gigs in the same venue from Black Sabbath to Stiff Little Fingers, leaving our ears buzzing with white noise. More comical as a venue was Rugby Theatre, a white-washed amateur redoubt, its stage breadth and proscenium arch ill-fitted to Panavision masterpieces such as *2001: A Space Odyssey* (1968). Kubrick's meticulous architectural compositions found themselves humbled by the abbreviated frame of the stage, slow-mo spaceships performing an ungainly wobble as they progressed over a kink at the edge of the screen. Nonetheless his films hang over the decade as implacable defining events, epic in scale and icy in tone. Even as mainstream cinema declined, prestige event films maintained their eminence.

For Paul and me, film had become about transgression, its certification as our target and challenge: we sought the most graphic violence, the most explicit sex. Roger Corman graduates such as Scorsese and de Palma brought together high intent and low violence, pushing codes of representation to breaking point; but my especial hero, Nicolas Roeg, spliced genre with avant-garde chronology and lubricious eroticism and his Britishness bridged the gap between us and the films we watched even while their stories were relentlessly displaced in focus.

Roeg's avatars offered escape from the fixed identities of nation, class and gender which dominated our lives. From Mick Jagger in *Performance* (1970) to the fluid figure of Donald Sutherland in *Don't Look Now*, climaxing in the hairless androgyny of Bowie in *The Man Who Fell to Earth* (1976), splashed with milk, probed and scanned and deeply objectified, Roeg's men travelled beyond conventional gender codes, rendered vulnerable. Bowie's Thomas Newton, slippery and pale, the end point of this process, and fed back into the very persona of the '*thin white Duke*' he adopted in place of 'rockist' machismo, becoming a sleek, ungainly European mystery with his relocation to Berlin. In a school where tradition was everywhere asserted and our cultural horizon was bounded by sleepily taught Shakespeare and Jane Austen, the cult film and the cult of film defined our conflicted pubescent selves, our voices plunging, our bodies suddenly hairy and coarse, our faces covered in zits; and our class identities mutating too, leaving us in a strange cynical space where we grew incomprehensible to our parents and to ourselves.

But the school itself was also a place of film; our film society, which was student-run, took over the cavernous space of Big School once a week after hours, a huge cloth screen covered the dais, the projector loaded with spools whirring in the dark, and the site of daily abasement was turned into something rich and strange. Much of it was crowd-pleasing stuff, Mel Brooks comedies or Monty Python. But then there was a revelatory screening of *O Lucky Man!* (1973), Lindsay Anderson's sprawling three-hour picaresque satirical road movie tracking the electrifying Malcolm McDowell as a coffee salesman traversing through the guts of class-bound technocratic Britain, accompanied by the musical commentary of Alan Price. If nothing else, with that pedigree, it was an induction into theatre as much as film.

Not all of *O Lucky Man!* has worn well – as McDowell follows his snakes and ladder trajectory into and out of the ruling class, the tone shifts between cod horror, sci-fi, Brechtian parable, social realism and road movie; but this eclecticism compounded its appeal as it offered an audit of all the forms of story I had consumed. The cast is a roll call of British theatrical talent, with figures familiar from television such as Arthur Lowe, James Bolam and Geoffrey Palmer, jostling against newcomers like Helen Mirren and knights of the stage like Ralph Richardson, playing her rapacious capitalist father. Roles were doubled which deepened the defamiliarising shock of this, with Lowe at one point adopting blackface to impersonate a stereoptyped African dictator.

Anderson, a great theatre director and film critic, working with screenwriter David Sherwin, was eking out his own film language. The film is shot through with allusion: Godard's own broken documentary on the Rolling Stones One Plus One – Sympathy for the Devil (1969) emulated in the footage of Alan Price and band; Anderson's deployment of the wintry gaze of Czech cinematographer Miroslav Ondricek mirrors his admiration of Ondricek's fellow countryman Milos Forman. Outside of Monty Python this was the first time I witnessed avant-garde and meta-cinematic effects: the use of interrupting text, irising, the 'limbo' scenes where Price and his band played, McDowell auditioning for the very film in which he stars, Anderson playing himself, patrician and chic in his leather jacket, beating him over the head with a script. Yet all of this was achieved in a studied and austere and very British way, slow-moving, inhabited by long silences and a rapt view of landscape.

The more the film drew attention to itself as film, the more its inner theatricality was made visible – and having consumed films as artefacts and end products, these interruptions and glimpses into the mechanism were a revelation. Its spirit was rooted in Anderson's desire for a production company which enabled an ensemble approach, unthinkable in British cinema at that time. The returning collaborators (Sherwin, McDowell, Ondricek, the designer Jocelyn Herbert who dominated the aesthetic of the Royal Court Theatre Anderson then presided over) permitted an almost improvised aesthetic, shifting and changing according to shot and context. Out of that familiarity came the bold grace notes of this strange movie.

Equally it was the first inkling of a politicised account of the country I was living in, a sense confirmed years later when I finally saw its superior predecessor If . . . . (1968) which exactly captured the destructive incubation of cynicism of my schooling experience. McDowell's Mick Travis, a new alter ego, effortlessly displaced Michael York's agreeable charm with his soft-voiced faintly northern menace, girlish wide eyes, insouciant gaze and sexual ambivalence. McDowell seemed to know things, with a quality of amorality powerfully deployed by Kubrick in A Clockwork Orange (1971) (and already out of circulation by then) and an air of danger that surely informed John Lydon's piss-taking leer. As Raymond Durgnat wrote, he had a 'post-Finney face', malleable enough to carry the film's transformations as he sidles up and down the class ladder. Not the sort of actor my dad would like, too hard to place in terms of class and intent, he embodied sly cleverness, a true grammar school trait I was cultivating. His detachment illuminates Anderson's shapeless, fascinating film, and accounted for my own intimations of feeling déclassé in a rigidly hierarchical world.

But the real revelation of the Sheriff film society came the day someone had the bright idea of projecting *Nosferatu The Vampyre* by Werner Herzog, shortly after its release in 1979.

Oh my God, that was an epiphany. Here was film as ART! Here was my entry ticket into the Art House. Here was what critic David Bordwell dubbed the genre of the 'Art film' motivated not by plot and box office but by, '*realism and authorial expressiveness*'.

It was the German-language version of the film and I was studying German, gripped by its sounds, besotted with the whistling idiom of my teacher Frau Dunn. I had read Bram Stoker and watched numerous Draculas; I thought I knew what this might be. But as the mystic warmth of Popol Vuh's soundtrack played over the somnambulistic images of Delft, as Bruno Ganz's vigilant Jonathan Harker made his way towards the castle where Klaus Kinski (whom Herzog dubbed '*my best fiend*') awaited him, bald as Bowie's alien, spindly fingers, glowing dark eyes, comically soft mouth ingratiating and strange, I was transported.

Herzog is unapologetic in his engagement with art history, unleashing the repertoire of German Romanticism from Caspar David Friedrich to F. W. Murnau in order, as he commented himself, to find a relationship with the past unavailable to his '*fatherless generation*'. Jorg Schimdt-Reitman's images are tableau-like in their contemplative distance, tracking Isabelle Adjani's Lucy as she progresses through Bosch-like disorder in Delft ('*the town is beginning to lose its moorings*'). As the image becomes the ascendant, plot recedes, and the act of looking replaces the processing of story.

Every shot conveys that felt response to landscape so central to all Herzog's work confirming André Bazin's sense that film creates a '*dramaturgy of Nature*', by which it fundamentally differentiates itself from theatre. As he notes in 'Theatre and Film' in film, '*the mainspring of the action is nature not man*'. Herzog's feeling for wildness and the visceral power of experiencing nature, derived perhaps from his film-free Bavarian childhood, banishes the stuffy hermetic world of the horror film. The very process of writing in advance of and through film is apparent in his process, with his prose scenarios standing in for conventional screenplays, terse literary works in their own right. Take his account of night in the Carpathian Mountains where, '*the moon rolls like a heavy wheel through murky clouds*'; or the ravine Harker passes through, where Herzog comments, '*mortal fear hovers*'.

Yet for me the star of the film was not Klaus Kinski's vampire but Bruno Ganz, his victim, now my new screen crush. Ganz offered the possibility of male gentleness, depth and intellectual curiosity without any need to assert itself. Ganz simply watches; his eyes know things; his crumpled nose suggests experience. Then there's his soft, deliquescent voice – such an irony that he became reduced in the minds of so many to Hitler's tizzy in *Downfall*, when here, or in Wim Wenders's masterly *The American Friend* (1977) or *Der Himmel über Berlin* (1987), his key note is compassionate reverie. Ganz is the perfect counterpoint to Hopper's frenzy in the former film and Kinski's theatricality in *Nosferatu*.

The Germany of the 1970s was somehow congenial to me; I'd been on an exchange to Russelsheim near Frankfurt where I stayed with a family of Opel workers whose son had the faintly comic name of Norbert Finger. This stay in the warm Rhenish lands, right at the summit of the West German economic miracle, in a landscape I would later recognise especially in the films of Wenders or in Edgar Reitz's *Heimat* (1984), opened up Europe in general, and Germany in particular, as somewhere that embraced modernity by necessity, that had wired class consciousness out of its sense of itself. It was somewhere comfortable with ideas too, and riven of course by terror at this time in the form of groups such as the Red Army Faction (the Baader-Meinhof Gang); a reality brought home to me by *The Lost Honour of Katharina Blum* by Volker Schlondorff and Margaretha von Trotta (1975).

It was Herzog and European film that really seized me in Big School in that darkness, transported from a place of polished wood and Oxbridge success stories and the boring ramblings of masters. No cheap sensation. No seeking to please me in any way. Performances that masked feeling to stir it more deeply. The painterly crepuscular images and meditative pace mesmerised me, even as I joined in with the groans as the film slipped off its spool and the screen became mere grainy white glare. I think many of us in that room that day were puzzled and bored by it at times. There's little direct fear, lots of dark Teutonic wit and the long stare of Herzog's documentary gaze at what he views. But *Nosferatu* inducted me into a world of film my parochial viewing could never have permitted me.

I count this as the beginning of my education.

4 *Solaris*: Learning to Dream

(DUNCHURCH)

EXT. A COUNTRY LANE, THE MIDLANDS. DAY.
A YOUNG MAN hunched over racing bike handles,
wind riffling through hair, freewheels through a
deep lane.

There are moments in life – and film - that feel heightened, shot through with light, seem to take place in entirely fine weather. I think of the tracking shots of cyclists in Truffaut's short film *Les Mistons* (1957), the troublemakers of the title freewheeling through light and shade in pursuit of Bernadette Lafont in her summer chemise, the camera constantly in motion, the kids stripy with the zoetrope effects of the poplar-lined outskirts of Nîmes, rimmed in lens-flare.

And our move to the village of Dunchurch, south of Rugby, was a portal into a new landscape of freedom, girlfriends and adolescence proper. The woody grounds of Bilton Grange school, Southam Road, after the chip shop, tapering to the rise of Toft Hill, where Draycote Reservoir flashes in the light, and we stayed out all night drinking cider; or the coaching house of the Dun Cow pub where we were merrily tolerated as underage drinkers; or the crumbling vicarage where my girlfriend – girlfriend! – Rhiannon lived with her bohemian family. I sewed my environs into a tapestry of sorties. And with these freedoms came new possibilities to create.

Cycling and film of course are contemporaries, and when cinema sets aside the car for the bike it achieves a kind of intimacy, whether in *Bicycle Thieves* (1948), *Lacombe Lucien* (1974), *Breaking Away* (1979), *Cyclo* (1995) or *Archipelago* (2010). Gone were dark journeys by bus, incubators of bullying; now I speed up the Dunchurch Road into town, double back down Hillmorton Road; the bike takes me from party to party, weaving in and out of town and outskirts. Rugby feels less inert somehow; life feels suddenly supple. There're no bike helmets, rarely even lights (which gets me into trouble with the police) – the wind's in your hair, and Warwickshire's mild undulations give you the thrill of freewheeling with little labour of ascent.

Dad's rise up the managerial ladder had earned us this relocation into a suburb masquerading as a village, in a tidy estate of new builds, lacking in ghosts, bullies or malevolent locals. It was official – we were middle class! And with the jettisoning of half of the school population after O Levels and the accession of sixth form privileges, Sheriff had changed from compulsion to somewhere more playful, a place of agency rather than duress. Needless to say, these new freedoms (free periods!) generated a concomitant quality of arrogance in me. I was released to become pretentious; where once a polysyllabic word would bring down the scorn of my peers in that manner well caught in the classic sociological work *Learning to Labour* (1970) by Paul Willis, your peers policing any hint of aspiration, now it granted you admiration – indeed you could revel in being 'weird', *outré,* experimental in utterance and action. A new culture of 'intellectual' display seemed acceptable, which as Dan Fox argues in *Pretentiousness* (2016) is the first vital gesture against class fixity.

My hair grew shaggier, I once tried to dye it with red paint to a predictably messy effect, I shaved off my sideburns and acquired a mass of compressed curls that earned me the nickname '*cabbage-head*' from less friendly quarters. I dumped my collection of sci-fi and horror like I shed my prog rock LPs in a Stalinist purge. Overnight 'Yes' were replaced by 'Talking Heads' as the logo on my rucksack. I dabbled in Kafka not Tolkien, I pretended to read Joyce. I didn't write; or rather I did, by joining a band.

Being in a band in the early 80s was hardly a rare experience and Rugby was thick with them. I summarily replaced the lead singer of an outfit of friends called 'Downfall' who I saddled with the more pretentious name of 'Dark Pop'. Musically illiterate, as Mark E. Smith said of his role in The Fall, I '*played my brain*'. It was a basic line-up – drums, Pete 'Fango' Franklyn, by far the finest instrumentalist among us whose hero was Buddy Rich but from whom we mainly wanted four-to-the-floor; the bassist Chris 'Horse' Leggatt, and with me the keenest to push the band from punk towards the lyricism of Joy Division or Echo and the Bunnymen; on guitar, curly-haired son of a Hungarian publican, Craig Sipos, a rockist riffer who adored little-known punk outfit Slaughter and the Dogs, an outfit as subtle as their name, and who only approved of my role in the band, '*cos Wally comes in on time and buys his own gear*'. And yes, me on vocals and indeed chief lyricist, my songs seeking to offer political critique ('Breaking Point' addressed the 1981 riots with little direct experience), literary musing ('Estranged' a rewrite of Erich Maria Remarque) and spurned-lover maunderings ('Waiting' which essentially rehearsed my irritation at not getting called back by my then girlfriend). These 3-minute wonders of self-pitying storytelling released me into the role of writer/performer.

The Rugby 'scene' meant the usual round of gigs at working men's clubs, the local Tech, church halls and mistakenly at Sheriff itself where we were denounced by our headteacher Geoffrey Martindale as the creators of '*animal noises*'. In my loose Army and Navy sage-green shirt, heavy DDR greatcoat, baggy cargo pants and tie knotted round my head I was a cut-price amalgam of Julian Cope, Billy Mackenzie and Ian McCulloch. But we had a set, we wrote songs recorded in dingy music studios, we cut a demo at the Long Buckby sound studio, sent it to John Peel, never heard back; we even had followers. And one of our rival bands, The Spacemen, peddlers of stoned-out feedback noise, featured one Jason Pierce, who went on to great success with Spiritualised. Jason, a likeable younger fellow Laurentian, lent me Stooges LPs, modelling himself on the gawky Iggy Pop that graced the cover of 'The Idiot'. Yes, the music scene, a deadly serious largely male affair, granted us artistic agency, and on rare occasions the odd bit of cash to supplement my job in the produce department of Sainsbury's where, in my brown polyester overcoat unloading bananas most Saturdays, I sabotaged any glamour acquired elsewhere.

I was taking possession of a new middle-class identity without apology, symptomatic of those early years of Thatcherism documented by Andy Beckett in *Promised You a Miracle* (2016). Indeed, with the jettisoning of my prog rock credentials for the snarky beadiness of the new wave this tendency was encouraged. As Simon Reynolds observes in *Rip it Up and Start Again* (2005) the transition from punk's nihilism to new wave's catholicity, yielded an entrepreneurial energy that mirrored Thatcher's assault on collectivism. Punk after all had been the last nail in the coffin of class deference. It was around this time that my parents, themselves life-long Labour supporters, jumped ship from the ailing party of Michael Foot to join the newly formed Social Democratic Party (SDP) launched in 1981 (a moment I explored in my play *Limehouse* (2017) many years later). The SDP wished to situate themselves in that very same new entrepreneurial space, in the process inventing a middle-class technocratic electorate that had yet to exist. Perhaps if it hadn't been for the Falklands War and the first-past-the-post system they might have succeeded.

I berated them for this at the time, but this defection had been a long time coming. Dad's socialism had been tested to destruction in his battles with militancy at Rolls Royce; now balding on top but graced with a lustrous dark beard, he was dubbed '*The Ayatollah*' by his workers and not in a good way, given the advent of Khomeini's theocratic republic in Iran. Timing loo breaks, stopping boozy Friday lunches, seeking to raise productivity levels, he met with rancour on the shop floor and pusillanimity from his line managers. For him the trade unions had sabotaged their party in the Winter of Discontent – but he couldn't countenance the Tories in any form and especially under Thatcher.

Mum's politics were always harder to call; if she'd been born a decade later she would have been a feminist. Certainly she called out sexism wherever she saw it, drilling me into my share of housework, dubbing dad an MCP, '*male chauvinist pig*'. Her move into the public sector had led her too back to seeking the education denied her as a girl, studying for a Social Work diploma in Wolverhampton, leaving us to fend for ourselves which generally meant nights of burnt fishcakes prepared by my poor sister. But mum was dealing with her own demons too, as her past resurfaced.

In the late 70s, Molly divorced Jack who dwindled into an early alcohol-induced death. After his funeral, with typical abruptness a letter arrived for mum in which Molly accounted for the circumstances of her birth. Not a telephone call, not a heart to heart, a letter. I still find this coolness astonishing, an emotional reserve she transmitted to mum, who, having rarely been loved, now hated to be touched, flinching at unbidden contact. In the letter Molly dropped her bomb; mum was not Jack's child. Her conception and birth took place during one of his long terms of wartime absence on a merchant navy vessel. Equally shocking, the embryonic Yvonne was a Londoner, conceived during the Blitz; and, most astonishingly of all, that her father was an unnamed Canadian GI.

Why was Molly in London? Had she fled the home in Portsmouth? It appeared she might be a hairdresser there – or maybe he was the hairdresser! Who our grandfather was is lost to us; back then Molly was tight-lipped, mainly that mixture of shame and reserve that stifled so many mid-century lives. As the bombs fell and she entered her third trimester, Molly was evacuated to Wiltshire to give birth. The father was never heard of again; was his Canadianness the source of mum's being named after Yvonne de Carlo, his countrywoman? Writing this I shared what I knew with my sister and even our accounts didn't align; I'd heard he'd died during a night of bombing which obliterated great swathes of London; she thought it had simply been a one-night stand.

Behind us lie years of disputed lineage. Dad's father Cecil (Cyril?) was adopted by a family at the end of the war, brought up as a Catholic, his own step-parents unknown, as he refused to maintain contact with them. My sense of displacement and disconnection from where I lived, even the country I was part of, had deep genetic roots it seemed. More freedom perhaps – but freedom has its cost. Behind us lay, it seemed, only mystery and silence.

The effects on mum of this revelation were hard to gauge, although five years later, after Molly's own early death of a stroke in Australia, she succumbed to a depression; she was a stranger to herself, displacing her confused feelings into a firestorm of activity, restless, unsentimental, viewing outsiders with a cold eye of amused fascination, a vantage point which may lie behind my own turn to writing.

Yet in 1981 while her expressing of love through deeds – knitting, cooking, making and mending – may have remained manic, her demeanour was more centred, not least because of our more secure social standing summed up in the endless dinner parties in which horrific quantities of food and drink were consumed in a kind of potlatch worthy of Mike Leigh's *Abigail's Party* (1977).

So even as the assault of the neoliberalism commenced, I can't help but see this time as a hopeful one. One portent of that was the changing place of television in my sentimental cinematic education marked by the founding of Channel 4 in 1982. Television is the subtext of so much of this cultural *Bildungsroman*; after all we consumed most of our films and drama on the small screen, notably the Plays for Today of Trevor Griffiths, David Mercer and above all Dennis Potter, whose 1976 *Pennies from Heaven* married the pleasures of film, theatre and the musical. Now Channel 4 seemed to offer a new access point to intellectual life unleashed from the paternalism of the BBC and with it a new postmodern energy.

Under its first controller Jeremy Isaacs, the new channel defined its remit as extending representation, inaugurating a new politics of identity and multiculturalism – and also to '*encourage innovation and experiment . . .*', an intellectual mandate epitomised by Michael Ignatieff's uncompromising late-night chat show '*Voices*' which confronted me with Umberto Eco or Susan Sontag. Equally bold was the foundation of Film on Four which set out to counter the famous canard of François Truffaut that there was an incompatibility between British life and cinema. As he observed to his hero Hitchcock, '*I get the feeling that there are national characteristics*

– among them the English countryside, the subdued way of life, the stolid routine – that are antidramatic in a sense.' As a survey of British cinema by James Park from 1984 noted, Film on Four's task would be 'learning to dream'. Yet as David Thomson points out in his seminal Biographical Dictionary of Film (1975), British television had long harboured extraordinary cinematic talents: Stephen Frears, Alan Bennett (who my mum adored), Alan Clarke. In Britain, to be an auteur was not a career option; the director was a humble craftsman and the screenwriter too often saw the screen as second best from the stage; Film on Four changed that equation.

For me the most enduring encounter on the new channel was from further afield: the films of Russian director Andrey Tarkovsky, devoured in one late-night Channel 4 season. For much as I was thrilled by cinema that might speak of our lives, Herzog had confirmed the medium as the source of adventure and difference. And Tarkovsky offered an arcane body of work closer to poetry and dream than drama. In my new persona, I had the courage to claim what that amounted to. And I was not alone; my new friend Stephen Meek, a 'commoner' at Rugby School no less, whose house, one street from Sheriff, was a haven of cultural experiment, with his corridors of vinyl (Dylan, Love, The Fall), his literary confidence (Gide, Hesse). Together we rose to the challenge of Tarkovsky. Given the films tended to go out late this involved the exercise of real willpower, each movie seen through dozings off as we were yet to have VCRs or DVDs to hand. We leaned over our small screens in order to enter the great epic spaces of Stalker (1979) or Solaris (1972) as an act of sheer endurance. But that was the point; this stuff was difficult! And the fact it was so forbidding was our route to genuine 'cultural capital', cred, taste or what Pierre Bourdieu would call 'distinction'. Resisting the impulse to switch off or drop off, mainlining Tarkovsky would be our rite of passage.

But what else kept us watching? Geoff Dyer recalls that on his first encounter with Stalker, in his wonderful Zona (2012), 'I was slightly bored and unmoved . . . I wasn't overwhelmed . . . but it was an experience I couldn't shake off.' Solaris too is burned into my memory even though I first watched it through a squint-hole like the portals on its eponymous space station; but it was the contrast between its elusive ideas and the distressed reality of its hardware that helped locate it in a tradition of space travel figured in entropic grimy naturalism, comically in John Carpenter's Dark Star (1974) and tragically in Douglas Trumbull's Silent Running (1972). Solaris shared their trapped air of boredom and drift, of eco-anxiety, as if colonising space merely continued the ravaging of the terrestrial realm. Nella Formina the costume designer noted that Tarkovsky disavowed any visual futurism, adopting the tired spacesuits of the tarnished Soviet era; the film's hero Kris Kelvin's most memorable costume element is his string vest.

Solaris is fused for me with another movie that haunts this period and defined the limits of the medium: Coppola's Apocalypse Now! (1979), seen at Rugby Town Hall, this time with helicopters wobbling over that pesky proscenium arch. Coppola's film came front-loaded with hooks, hitting the zeitgeist with relish, generating a psychedelic revival, thanks to The Doors's 'The End' doomily washing in and out of the soundtrack, its paraphernalia informing the Bunnymen's live show with their camo-nets, or McCulloch's scouse reworking of Morrison's drawl. Again, design was foremost in our response – the worn paraphernalia and distressed uniforms as significant as the anti-war narrative. And for all the operatic splendour of Vittorio Storaro's images the film has the same entropic structure that Tarkovsky deploys to critique the so-called Hero's Journey, which, thanks to writer Christopher Vogler, was about to become Hollywood's template.

But there are other odd parallels between the films. Donatas Banionis's Kris in *Solaris* and Martin Sheen's Willard in *Apocalypse* resemble each other in their taciturn asexuality. They are both numb organisation-men, pure-hearted yet damaged knights of the Grail, too traumatised to speak, wrapped up in 'characterless' stoicism. Kris begins his story with self-deprecation: '*I am not a poet. I have never moved anyone with words. Perhaps that's why they chose me.*' Likewise, Willard, going insane in his Saigon hotel room, muses, '*Everyone gets everything he wants. I wanted a mission. And for my sins they gave me one.*'

Both men are summoned to undertake a quest they barely understand which takes them into a territory that unravels them further. And both films take the quest genre and steadily dismantle it, turning journeys up-river or into the depths of space into journeys into memory and the self, collapsing into hallucinogenic introspection. That seemed to chime with our new freedoms as we were hurtled into the experiments of the 1980s.

Seeing Tarkovsky's work at the height of what was called by Chomsky and others the Second Cold War had another effect. It made it harder to reduce the menace we were encouraged to detect in the USSR to faceless malice. Tarkovsky's exile in the late 70s as Soviet chief artistic dissident after Solzhenitsyn (a role he rejected) complicated that, and he seemed to sum up a deep Russian national mysticism as much as the charms of Western capitalism. His relocation to Italy and Sweden under the tenure of his mentor Ingmar Bergman seemed a significant stepping away from the bipolar conflict; his motherland having, he claimed, rendered him a '*zero*' by suppressing his great film *Andrei Rublev* (1966). All Tarkovsky's films are shot through with exile and ecological yearning – the opening of *Solaris* could hardly be further from the machine cult of shiny sci-fi, as Vadim Yusov's camera gazes at Tarkovsky's perennial motifs of weed shivering in a flowing stream or the frenzied gallop of a horse. In the heart of the space station, stalked by the simulacrum of his dead wife, Kris's meditations yield a long rostrum shot across Breughel's 'The Hunters in the Snow' as Bach's 'Ich Ruf Zu Dir, Herr Jesu Christ' plays (I gained my education in classical music from Tarkovsky and Kubrick (Ligeti, Bartok)). His apparent return is only one more solipsistic delusion as we pull away with painful slowness from his childhood dacha to find it confounded in the sea of memory dominating this planet of ache.

Yusov described working on the film, '*an endless search and a trial*'; that also describes the film itself. It inducted me into a new tempo of drama, where slowness meant not boredom but intensity and rapture, with fast cutting disavowed as one more concession to attention-deficit narratives. With only the slightest of camera movement, images register time in small shifts and changes and the viewer becomes literally transfixed; as Tarkovsky puts it, film is *'sculpting in time'*.

Tarkovsky's greatest work is *Mirror* (1975); here all his contradictory impulses assemble in an unclassifiable essay-memoir-poem centred on his childhood and his mother's experiences, evoking the tragedy of twentieth-century Soviet history. As in *Solaris* there are traces of genre in here with moments that wouldn't be out of place in a horror film: a woman forces a boy to read out a letter by Pushkin only to vanish, leaving traces of her coffee's heat-mark on a table. Oneiric images of fire are framed from within a house dripping in paradoxical rain, the mother's wet hair uncoiling like the snakes from Medusa's head. Every moment in this prism of a film is charged with a significance it refuses to disclose but which is felt in the viewer's body. As Tarkovsky notes, it deploys an *'associative logic of music or poetry'*. Yet his private hermeticism is spliced with epic hints of history. Had I seen it in 1981 *Mirror* would have baffled and repelled me; but I was edged into his aesthetic by the guiding wheels of genre which make *Solaris* a film I remember as an induction but don't wish to rewatch.

Coppola's film also undermined cold-war antimonies in a more hectic way despite the gung-ho tendencies of screenwriter John Milius, as Jimmy Carter's liberal turn succumbed to Reagan's hawkism. It marks the swansong of a decade of American dissent and experiment; the madness of its making is brilliantly captured in *Hearts of Darkness* by his wife Eleanor Coppola (1991), pushing the studio system to the point of collapse, mimetic of the very colonial war it critiques. Yet it would give way to the non-reflexive pieties of *Platoon* and 80s cinema's retreat into likeable genre, teen movies and animation. Its very chaotic qualities embodied its own internal confusion and spoke deeply to our unformed teenage minds.

Rugby was located deep in this climate of dread, not least because of the appurtenances of the Cold War and our own military-industrial complex. After all my dad's job was part of that, with Rolls Royce serving military as much as civilian purposes, machine tools creating weapons of war exported to future enemies such as Iraq. One reason for his giving up on Labour was what he perceived as the pacifism of Michael Foot or Tony Benn. We lived under the shadow of a weapon delivery system guided by those innocuous radio masts, serving newly installed Polaris and Cruise missiles confirming our slavish relationship to the United States.

This centrality was confirmed when the Campaign for Nuclear Disarmament held a huge rally in Brownsover north of Rugby, after marching to those masts winking in the night. Canon Bruce Kent spoke out and The Beat played. It was my first political rally and it broke apart the frozen politics of the time, offsetting nights of bad dreams generated by 'Protect and Survive' pamphlets.

Two other odd coincidences changed my perception of myself and my future. One was the Granada TV production of Evelyn Waugh's *Brideshead Revisited* in 1981, elegantly adapted by John Mortimer and Charles Sturridge which set me off into the class-riddled thickets of the mid-century English novel and established the notion of Oxford, before merely a pretty Cotswold town to me, as an Arcadian destination.

University itself was a mystery to me – my sister had just made it to Sheffield, the first of us to take up a degree, in her case Chemistry. Sheffield, exiting from industrialism, was an exciting destination for me, getting off with her older friends on its cold dark streets, going to gigs in the abandoned works of the Leadmill, seeing Howard Barker's *A Passion in Six Days* (1983) in the Crucible, a scathing account of a Labour Party conference which inducted me into the excitements of socialist theatre. But what allowed me to dare to dream to apply to Oxford was a talk at one of our interminable speech days by old Laurentian Dr Valentine Cunningham, speaking on the theme of 'waste'. His zany subversive text linked the local sewage works with Dickens's *Hard Times* thereby mounting a devastating attack on Thatcher's use of unemployment as a political tool. This goon-voiced, unassuming orator blew apart what I imagined an Oxbridge don might be – and despite my patchy three A Levels of History, English and Economics I resolved I would take what was then called '*seventh term*' entry.

Suddenly I was being encouraged to see myself as someone who *thought*. It brought me in to close acquaintance with that very same headteacher, Geoffrey Martindale, who'd written off my punk efforts but now invited me into his sepulchral study to discuss Joseph Conrad, pressing on me his personal copy of F. R. Leavis's *The Great Tradition*. I found Leavis's prim reduction of the entirety of English Literature to eight writers repellent, and yet I couldn't deny the weight he granted literature in a world without God – a seriousness reflected in Mr Martindale.

The humourless figure rebuking us from the dais day after day, close to, was a generous thinker, granting me terrifying silences into which I released my confused thoughts, which he would sift with a shocking degree of respect. I'd heard that in his youth he'd been captured by the Japanese in Burma, immured in a prisoner-of-war camp as brutal as those in David Lean's *The Bridge on the River Kwai* (1957) or more saliently Nagisa Oshima's *Merry Christmas, Mr Lawrence* (1983). His guarded civility, his deep reverence for literature seemed grounded in something painful carried forward from that time. I felt I was in the presence of someone of deep liberality; and the permissive silence he left for me to fill was a terrifying space of responsibility as much as freedom. He weighed his words; could I do likewise?

I made my application; one day a brown letter arrived inviting me to interview. I went to Corpus Christi College, Oxford, where the very same Dr Cunningham sat opposite me. I worried mum because I turned up late to the wrong interview in my bright-green new Benetton jumper. But then two weeks later as snow fell and Christmas arrived, another letter arrived.

Its content was reported in the local paper *The Rugby Advertiser* in an article simply entitled 'To Oxford'; the article went on, '*Steve Waters, a former student at Lawrence Sheriff better known as lead singer in Dark Pop and employee at J. Sainsbury's has been granted an Exhibition Scholarship to Corpus Christi College Oxford to study English Literature and Language.*'

But first I would go to Israel.

5 *Shoah*: Living Dangerously

(ISRAEL)

EXT. KIBBUTZ DALIA. MAY, 1984. NIGHT
  The dark air is like silk. On a hill's rise in the Sports Stadium, a film plays under a violet sky, lighting up hundreds of faces: Israelis, Arabs, Druze, and British, Swedish, Swiss, German and Italian volunteers.

I am with them, watching the lush richly colourised images of Francis Ford Coppola's doomed reinvention of the musical *One from the Heart* (1981); Tom Waits and Crystal Gayle, the voices of Frederic Forrest and Terri Garr, rebound off the soft wooded hills of Ramot Menashe, the '*place of the winds*', in Megiddo, 10 miles in from Haifa. Forty miles north the fall-out of Menachem Begin's assault on southern Lebanon plays out, which three years earlier provoked a systematic slaughter of Palestinian refugees in the camps of Sabra Shatila by Israel's Phalangist allies – an atrocity captured decades later in *Waltz with Bashir* (2008).

  The confused erotic feelings of that night and others like it – the feeling of being at home in a place that was far from home and emphatically not my home; the entry into sexual experience that occurred in confused and apparently risk-free ways – seem to define the real beginning of adulthood for me, in a rush of intoxicating freedom.

  It's hard not to see this as a match cut, one of those exhilarating moments in films where montage takes us from one state to another. The splice from the long last day before call-up in a small Polish American town in Pennsylvania to the shocking violence of Vietnam in Michael Cimino's *The Deerhunter* (1978). The match cut between a bone tossed into the air by an ape on the verge of evolution to the spinning orbit of a spaceship in Kubrick's *2001*, thrilling in its omission of transition. In memory life is one cut after another and the shock of jumping from Warwickshire to a nation being built in real time in the Middle East is inevitably filmic.

  Why I am here is laughably arbitrary. I am not Jewish nor am I Arabic. I have no claim on the region nor reason to be there. But this was the era of gap-year adventure and one clear prospect was to be a volunteer on a Kibbutz.

  Just as my family had no history in higher education they also had few precedents for travel. Bar a holiday in Spain in 1971 where we spent our time on the standard package holiday in towering hotels, not at all mindful of Franco's regime, we never left the UK, except for one unhappy French exchange to the twin town of Evreux and the aforementioned trip to Russelsheim. Despite the merchant navy's role in my ostensible grandad's life, and Molly being born in Malta, the foreign was perceived through the lens of imperialism or as the dividend of the multicultural Midlands where several of my friends were of Ukrainian or Polish or Hungarian émigré families, escapees from communism. Abroad seemed very far away. But film offered a way there which didn't simply mean the USA where our imagination was encouraged to reside on a daily basis.

So I'd found myself in Hendon sitting at a briefing for British volunteers for the Kibbutz system, among kids with yarmulkes. And then I'd found myself on a plane for Tel Aviv arriving at Ben Gurion Airport on a warm velvety January night, driven on a minibus to a tiny community near Haifa, Kibbutz Dalia.

We carry latent myths within us. And for all my sense of myself then as rootless, not answerable to any past, I was here at the end point of centuries of colonialism which had shaped a template of the detached British traveller, entering other realities and leaving just as easily. It was an idea I'd absorbed from my reading: from Conrad's beady accounts of colonial outsiders in *Lord Jim* (1900) or *Nostromo* (1904), '*submitting to the destructive element*' or from Graham Greene, and perhaps especially his travelogue *Journey without Maps* (1936) or the recently filmed *The Honorary Consul* (1983) or the television adaptation of Paul Scott's *Raj Quartet,* 'The Jewel in the Crown' (1984). There, Charles Dance, in his shockingly white suit and tanned good looks, offered the archetype for the drink-sozzled outsider seeing out the Empire in melancholy luxury; further back is the even more dangerous example of my namesake T. E. Lawrence, the Colonel Kurtz of the Hashemites, crystallised in the image of Peter O'Toole's blindingly blue eyes locked onto the homoerotic gaze of Omar Sharif.

Years later I would recognise this archetype adapting Giles Foden's 1998 novel *The Last King of Scotland* for the stage in the figure of Nicholas Garrigan, the invented doctor, an amalgam of white British émigrés who stayed behind in Uganda during Idi Amin's terror; indeed my own play *World Music* (2003) was an attempt to analyse the White Saviour syndrome.

Yet back then, in my baggy Turkish pants, my olive tan and loose shirt I felt I was a citizen of the world. Like so many Zionist pioneers my lens was a European one; for me the key landmark of my shallow study of history was the Holocaust, unfolded in excruciating history lessons with our well-meaning teacher Mr Capewell, who showed us the 'Holocaust' mini-series when it was screened in 1978, with Meryl Streep carrying the moral weight of the Jewish community's fate, a role she reprised in Alan J. Pakula's dutiful version of William Styron's *Sophie's Choice* (1982). English-language filmic attempts to engage with these inconceivable events culminate in Spielberg's admirably stark *Schindler's List* (1993) reaching for singular stories and falling foul of the pornography of re-enactment.

The French tradition was different, rooted in the dark cloud of French complicity; *Nuit et Brouillard* (1956) by Alain Resnais acknowledges the shortfall between what is represented and what was experienced, with its asynchronous focus on the remnants of the camps in the present set against devastating footage of their past. Resnais, having worked in archival film, drew on a screenplay from a survivor of Mauthausen camp, Jean Cayrol. Their approach was to spatialise the film rather than employ narrative, with weary tracking shots mapping out traces of Auschwitz set against the dry voice-over of Michel Bouquet who asks, '*Is it in vain that we try to remember*?' (notably the German version of the film was translated by the great survivor poet Paul Celan). The present is in sharp colour; the past black and white. Resnais's unanchored voice-over creates another layer of irony, as if the film itself speaks. Even with its 30-minute running time Truffaut called it, '*the greatest film ever made*'.

I didn't have the benefit of Claude Lanzmann's *Shoah* to draw on, given his documentary corrective to anodyne engagements with the horrors of genocide only emerged in 1985. This nine-hour film (intended to be two!), eleven years in the making, testifies to film's role as both an account of history and a participant in it. As Lanzmann commented, '*it had to be difficult.*' *Shoah*'s terrible power rests in its refusal to resort to the archives, working from the present backwards, forcing the imagination to piece out what we are told, refusing the easy grace of the edit for the arduous work of memory in real time. This can make for a cruel watch as Lanzman drives survivors such as Abraham Bomba in an Israeli barbershop to relive his allocated task as barber in Treblinka, even after he pleads, '*Please don't make me go on.*' The film opens with Tarkovsky-like lyricism as we see a man glimpsed through trees singing as he's rowed along a river. He is Simon Srebnik returned from an Israeli Kibbutz to Chelmno in Poland, the camp now grassed over and shaded with encroaching trees. He walks along a dusty unmetalled road, face darkened by unreadable emotions; he stops and stares beyond the frame. This moment of unbearable tension is broken by his stony utterance, unthinkable in the calm: '*They burned a lot of people here. Yes, this is the place.*'

Constructed out of long scenes of narration, interview and translation, we find ourselves in the company of survivors, witnesses and perpetrators, compelled to piece their accounts together without the relief of montage, music or voice-over. This method bridges the gap between the contemplative present and the unimaginable horror of the past. To witness this over two long and arduous afternoons in a cinema forces the viewer to focus on faces and hands, the tics and gestures that television would lose. Whilst the project of Israel predated these events, the version I experienced in a community largely composed of Romanian migrants and their children, was indelibly formed by it.

The Kibbutz movement was congenial, rooted in the socialist values I adhered to, a practical version of communism which excited me as much as the exotic setting and a fusion of village and school. We shared meals in the dining hall, worked in the cool of the morning in citrus groves or late into the night in a soap powder factory. We all earned about £20 a month and this was common across the community. We were invited to take part in deliberations and debates; we received lectures about the Holocaust, the history of the region, the nefarious role of my countrymen during the Mandate. We celebrated Pesach and Yom Kippur, fell silent when the alarm sounded on Holocaust Day (Yom HaShoah); having done my Interrail and dutifully visited Dachau, I now went to Yad Vashem in Jerusalem. Nights without TV were spent playing chess, eating oranges, drinking coffee and diving in the communal swimming pool. It was a place of dark green cypress trees, golden hills under sprinklers, glittering fruit orchards, bone-white modernist buildings.

We lived and worked among survivors. I remember the elderly liver-spotted man working alone in the produce section. He said nothing to me as I arrived to gather supplies from the dry cool of the warehouse. He disappeared into its dark, leaving every door he passed through ajar, moving soundlessly about while I waited for him to load up my trolley before wheeling it to the communal kitchens. His spectral presence unnerved me; he looked through me and I felt stupidly disgruntled by that. I complained to Maddie, the vivacious Parisian cook who ran the kitchens. Her habitual smile vanished. She sat me down at the zinc workstation and baldly informed me this prematurely aged man had been in Auschwitz as a boy. While there, the authorities allotted him the task of closing the doors to the gas chambers, to provide a kind of specious calm to those being ushered to their deaths. In this very role, he had closed that heavy iron door on members of his own family. Now he could not, would not shut a door, any door.

His story was not atypical in Kibbutz Dalia.

We volunteers had little idea who we lived among. We were a miscellaneous bunch, ranging from unemployed punky English drifters, middle-class British Jewish kids seeking to connect with Zion, and fellow travellers from across Europe. We were left to our own devices in wooden huts like some strange scout camp with spiders and snakes and open fires. We spent nights pissed on arak; troublemakers were dealt with through kangaroo courts; it was more anarchism than communism. This fragile community found a storyteller in the shape of Paul Kember and his play *Not Quite Jerusalem* in 1984, adapted into a dire film by Lewis Gilbert. In shared huts we made love or tried to ignore others doing so and I read and read and read, fumbling my way out of the darkness of my ignorance into a historical tragedy that was not mine to claim.

This version of Israel was of course between the 1967 wars and the Oslo accords in the 90s, shortly before the first intifada of 1987. There was no Palestinian Authority or Gaza Strip; all were 'Occupied Territories'. The slightly aloof young adults who kept their distance from us, gorgeous corkscrew-haired Sabra women and physically assured young guys, were already doing military service, their version of Zionism stress tested. Dalia had an armed guard post; and yet the country was yet to succumb to waves of terror, although there had been assaults on the northern Kibbutzes. After the Camp David accords and the rapprochement between Begin and Sadat (who now had been assassinated), there was no imminent threat of invasion, although in the Golan Heights where I joined an archaeological dig, Hafez al-Assad's guns had only just fallen quiet. We were taken on a road trip led by a reckless Londoner called David, who led us into caves on the Lebanese border armed with an AK-47. In that wet darkness I didn't know whether to be more frightened of the bats shearing out of caverns or a lone PLO gunman as we broke surface in the low scrub of the disputed borderlands.

The freedom was electrifying. Young soldiers were given to hitching their way across the country and I hitched too, oblivious to risk. One day on Mount Carmel above Haifa I fell in step with a *keffiyah*-wearing Arab man, entering into one of those confused well-meaning exchanges of mimed gestures and jumbled words. He was a shepherd out on the scrubby heights, minding a handful of goats and sheep. He invited me into the pungent cave of his hut, hanging with fly-pleasing breads and spices. I sat on his diwan and gratefully ate his bread at which point he leaned in to kiss me. I recoiled in confusion, realising too late what his gestures of a finger jabbed repeatedly into a curved palm actually meant. I struggled free, took his picture and left. He must have thought me as stupid as I felt.

I drifted to Galilee, sleeping out in a Crusader castle harassed by mosquitoes, a scorched disciple in sandals and loose garb. I was drunk on experience and yet doomed to banality as I had no method to escape the prototypes that shaped everything I did as tourism. Yet these experiences made me imagine myself that most tarnished of words: an internationalist.

I had no inkling that at the edge of these experiences, ideologies that would define our lives were being incubated; this now seems a pause of innocence precisely because in this apparently bipolar world, it was possible to navigate place through values defined as right and left. With the advent of the next phase of the Cold War, client states and shifting geopolitics lit up scattered nations like a strange circuit board. I had little idea then of the centrality of American support in Israel and indeed its conflicts with its Arab neighbours would fuel Islamism even within the decade.

At this point the Israeli left and the 'Peace Now' movement created an apparent meeting point for some Palestinian activists such as Al-Fatah who considered themselves part of a wider leftist struggle against imperialism and received Soviet funding; the memory of Nasser's vision of pan-Arabism made the conflict no less deadly but less couched in irrationalism. And the left in general was only beginning to conceive of Israel in Third World-ist terms.

Likewise when I later travelled around Turkey still reeling from the 1980 coup, I never felt a sense of risk whether in the company of Kurdish rebels in the far east peering over the border at Dogubeyazit where Ararat rose and Soviet flags asserted control over the Armenian borderlands, Iranians and Iraqis and Kurds pouring over the border. I was peering into what would become the cauldron of the decades of conflict to come, seeing only antiquity and stability.

Most ironic of all was my tenure in Hungary and disappeared nations such as Yugoslavia just as they succumbed to the collapse of communism or the break-up of the federation in the most vicious conflict of the 1990s; by this time I imagined myself a communist and saw everything through the lens of confirmation bias, lecturing Hungarian kids itching for what they imagined capitalist freedom might look like about its downsides and the virtues of Marxist theorist Georg Lukacs. Even here film was not far away for I was in Gyula, a bleak remote border town hard against the disputed

Romania border, the setting of Bela Tarr's slow nightmare of a film *Satantango* (1994). My wanderlust sheltered within a protective ignorance in regions on the brink of shattering change.

I had a script for all this; the early 80s were marked by a genre of films where privileged Westerners flirted with disaster in conflict zones, summed up by the title of Peter Weir's archetypal *The Year of Living Dangerously* in 1982, with Mel Gibson and Sigourney Weaver falling in love against the backdrop – always that phrase – of Sukarno's coup in the Philippines. The defining version was Roland Joffe's factually based *The Killing Fields* (1984) where Sam Waterstone plays the obligatory liberal journalist trying to save his interpreter Dith Pran from the horrors of the Khmer Rouge regime, a more benign exploration of culpability, but as Spalding Gray, cast in a bit part in the film, explored in his comic monologue *Swimming to Cambodia* (1986), the scope of production seemed to reproduce the neocolonialism indicted. More interesting was Schlondorff and von Trotha's fine film *Die Falschung (Circle of Deceit)* (1981) centring on my erstwhile hero Bruno Ganz as yet one more correspondent, this time in Lebanon, and here there is less of the easy humanist optimism that tends to govern the genre.

Cinema is the global art form par excellence. Even if distributors flinch at it, subtitled films take us closer to other places and lives than any other art form. Theatre, even with surtitles, does not travel well; the work is seen through a gauze of distance. Novels and poetry lose their particularity in translation. Yet while we've all flinched at the crassness of subtitling, a film in a foreign language is available to us, as film is about so much more than language. The triumph of *Parasite* by Bong Joon-Ho winning Best Picture at the 2020 Oscars suggests this process might have moved to a whole new phase.

I have become a world citizen through cinema and cinema has produced waves of work inducting us into cultures and places we knew little of. The 20s was the decade of German and Soviet as much as American cinema; the 30s saw the consolidation of the French tradition just as the 40s the Italian not to mention Indian. The astonishing example of Bergman in the 50s and 60s moved the compass point north, or eastwards into Poland or Czechoslovakia; the German cinema returned in earnest in the 70s, with an explosion of film-making in the Global South. In recent years excitement and innovation are more likely to be discerned in Turkish, Iranian, Argentinian or Korean film than anywhere in Europe.

The provincialism of English-language film has been constantly pushed back on – and the intersection between travelling oneself and travelling within film is one constant in my adult experience. My journeys across the collapsing realm of the communist bloc in Europe primed me for the films of Holland, Kieslowski, Zanussi, Szabor, Jancso and the like. My travels across the body of Turkey into Eurasia ignited my appetite for the films by Guney, then later the masterly films of Nuri Bilge Ceylan or indeed the nearby tradition of cinema in Iran from Kiarostami to Farhadi. And this breach of my provincialism begins in 1984 with my six months in Israel/Palestine.

(OXFORD)

EXT. CORPUS CHRISTI COLLEGE, OXFORD. DAY.
A 16th-century quad of warped flagstones punctuated
by a sundial; we move past a secluded chapel and
hammer-beamed library to a walled garden, to see
beyond it the expanse of Christchurch Meadows and
slow spread of the Thames.

If Oxford taught me nothing else, it taught me to think and watch politically.

As with most experiences in my life I arrived in a state of radical innocence. I had
lucked into this world. It was another closed community; I seemed to progress
through them as through the layers of a Russian doll. Here students played at
parliamentarians in our weekly JCR (Junior Common Room) meetings, confrontational
affairs in a room full of cigarette smoke and yellowing newspapers, as we debated
how to spend our small budget. Improbably eloquent PPE students dominated,
among them the future lost leader of the Labour Party David Miliband, and a
Yorkshireman who went on to edit *The Mail on Sunday*. Every week we'd go armed
for some sort of showdown and my first misstep was instructive.

The Falklands War had concluded in victory for the now invulnerable Thatcher
government. In its wake the 'left faction' of the JCR had proposed sending a paltry
but symbolic sum of money in support of the 323 Argentinian victims of the SS
General Belgrano, infamously sunk by a British torpedo as it entered the so-called
Maritime Exclusion Zone around the islands. The sinking was of course an act of war
but what was in question was whether the ship was leaving or entering the zone at
the point it was torpedoed.

Perhaps a bunch of students in an Oxford common room were not brilliantly
placed to adjudge this fault line of military morality. I made my first contribution by
speaking against the motion, quoting ex-prime minister Jim Callaghan, my dad's
hero, to the effect that if he'd been there he'd have sunk it too. The ensuing outrage
from the very people I wanted to impress, the Left, astonished me. I'd no idea how
reactionary my centrist stance might seem to them. I can't remember if the vote still
passed but I certainly remember the exclusion zone that descended around me by
those who snubbed me as R. W: 'Right Wing'. Ouch! Slowly I crawled back into their
approval, voting in the following meeting to support a fighting fund for the National
Union of Mineworkers (NUM) as they dug in for their rearguard fight against pit

closures. But my first lesson at Oxford was to realise I was a political being, as capable of being deeply wrong as right.

It was symptomatic of a time when being *'ideologically sound'* was vital. The Left was on the back foot and incubating in universities what Robert Hughes would later call a *'culture of complaint'*. And it confirmed a deeper struggle within me as I sought to extirpate the legacy of uncritically absorbed ideas from my provincial past in the face of seductive intellectual discoveries challenging everything I knew. Central to this was something simply called 'Theory'. While Val Cunningham's relationship to this body of work was nuanced, my other tutor, Glaswegian Tommy Docherty, hotfoot from Roland Barthes's Paris, was an exciting vector of it, setting us puzzling tasks such as trying to find a link between Swift's *The Tale of a Tub* (1704) and Gilles Deleuze and Felix Guattari's incomprehensible anti-Freudian polemic *L'Anti-Oedipe* (1972); later, after we became friends, he admitted there probably wasn't one.

One strand was deep feminism, derived from French theorists such as Monique Wittig or Hélène Cixous which took the struggle against inequality into the terrain of meaning and language. Then there was queer theory, evident particularly in the writings of Michel Foucault and his *History of Sexuality* (1976) – that sexuality, something I'd frankly just ventured into, might have a history was a revelation in itself; being among 'out' gay men and women and working out where I was positioned on that spectrum was another instructive task. Post-structuralism in all its forms seeped into the small print of behaviour, striking at the stable male self I'd imagined I possessed. Dethroned from my *phallogocentrism* I sat in the library staring at a copy of Jacques Derrida's *Signsponge* (1984) realising I'd no idea what the marks on the page in front of me amounted to, but that somehow they mattered.

The third current was something I could cleave to more easily – Marxism, and in particular the so-called Frankfurt School in interwar Germany. Frederic Jameson's vital *Marxism and Form* (1971) inaugurated me into Adorno and Benjamin while alerting me to a key influence in my subsequent life, Bertolt Brecht. Marxism's chief advocate in Oxford at that time was Terry Eagleton, over at Wadham College, an unlikely revolutionary, wry, flat-voiced, jokey and dressed like a geography teacher. His *Literary Theory* (1983) offered the most lucid way into those debates and his lectures were witty acts of debunking. Eagleton was a magnet for young acolytes who dubbed themselves 'Oxford English Limited' (OEL), who sought to reform the thicket of tradition that was the English degree. For those of us defeated by irregular Anglo-Saxon verbs or skimming Henry James's incomprehensible late novels through the night, the idea of a further layer of intellectual toil seemed a mixed blessing.

At one OEL event I plaintively defended the status quo against their desire to junk literary studies to make room for all of the theory we'd have to study. An Eagleton apostle sneered that all literature from George Eliot to Beckett was merely documents of the bourgeoisie in crisis and could be despatched in a term. My unreformed soul recoiled from this Maoist certainty; I'd sit in on Eagleton's weekly reading groups only to be denounced calmly by him as a *'Left Pessimist'* for demurring from his pronouncements.

Yet somehow that strand of German Leftism stayed with me because it tessellated with my other excitement – an orgiastic engagement with film history. I was in a city where I could watch films around the clock at virtually no expense. Across the Cowley Road where I would *'live out'* in my second year was the legendary Penultimate Picture Palace (PPP). This was a refurbished version of the 1930s East Oxford Picture Palace, opened by Bill Heine and Pablo Butcher in 1974, its frontage painted black and adorned with Al Jolson hands. It offered a sense of fantasy on an otherwise dull side street twinned with the pink-fronted 'Not the Moulin Rouge' (NTMR) in Headington, where stockinged legs burst out of a pitched roof to the horror of Oxford planners.

NTMR was given over to contemporary arty movies like the modish films of Jean-Jacques Beneix, *Diva* (1981) and *Betty Blue* (1986), symptomatic of the rush towards empty *'cinematic'* value in the early 80s, all artifice and lush colour, with the aesthetic of an Athena calendar. The English-language equivalent was the work of Ridley Scott, also an advertising graduate. His sensorially enhanced cinematic language produced one masterpiece in the form of *Blade Runner* (1982) which I saw so many times I could recite David Webb Peoples's dialogue for Rutger Hauer fondling a dove in its ubiquitous rain. But for me the PPP was my schooling; here a headlong programme of classic film ran through the day and night, comparable to Langlois's legendary cinematheque in Paris which provided the crucial grounding in the past from which emerged the *nouvelle vague*.

Film history creates the present and future of film; a crucial lodestar for me was Philip French, chief movie critic for *The Observer* from the 60s to the 90s. French's elegant reviews located every release in a deftly sketched prehistory that illuminated the medium's constantly erased history. He had his biases: his Swedish heritage led him back again and again to Bergman, he cherished westerns whatever their quality, he would regular tick off art-house masterworks for their humourlessness. But he was also relentlessly fair in his scholarly expositions. Because of French I came out of *Performance* seeing the presence of Borges; because of French I looked again at David Fincher's *The Social Network* (2010) as a key work of the twenty-first century. He was not alone in this role; we'd grown up on Barry Norman's fatherly audits of new releases, or Derek Malcolm's internationalist outlook in the *Guardian*. I'd fossick through old editions of Pauline Kael or Andrew Sarris and be profoundly challenged by the sweeping judgements of David Thomson. All of them sought to place modern productions in a long, loving history of the medium which I could check out at the PPP.

An evening might go like this: 6 p.m. – *WR: Mysteries of the Organism,* (1971), Yugoslavia, director: Dusan Makavejev; 8 p.m. – *Theorem*, (1968), Italy, director: Pier Paolo Pasolini; 10 p.m. – *Partie de Campagne,* (1936), France, director : Jean Renoir. In that dark temple on Jeune Street the history of cinema awaited me night after night, week after week, for a pittance. Heine who died in 2019 shaped my life incalculably through transmitting his cineaste passions.

But the real confrontation was with feminism. I'd spent so much of my life grounded in homosocial and heterosexual enclaves; indeed, my engagement with women within culture – as writers, as artists, as musicians – was minimal. And this was especially true of the deeply masculine culture of film where the patriarchal director held sway, embodied in the shocking licence with which auteurs such as Godard, Bertolucci or Peckinpah would objectify the women in their lives and work. For the first time I was in the company of female peers who alerted me to the tacit misogyny informing the culture I consumed.

My own college only admitted women three years before my arrival and their minority status placed astonishing pressures on them as they asserted their right to be there both with their male peers and teachers. In the drama scene in which I began to dabble, cocky young men called the shots and I aimed to join their number. I was shocked into becoming a playwright by the annual Cuppers drama competition for which I penned a pastiche of the Anglo-Saxon I was failing to understand fused with a satire of NUM leader Arthur Scargill. I cast myself as the Scargill surrogate and doled out dubious puny roles for my peers such as Offa the Dyke or the Venerable Bore. Yet we found ourselves before a panel of the giants of the drama scene such as Patrick Marber and Katie Mitchell and our hastily assembled one-act play came a glorious second – I had become a kind of accidental playwright. Yet within that same scene I felt personally affronted by the women-only endeavours Mitchell and others were creating, her consciousness-raising women-only theatre company Medusa, confronting me with a male privilege I'd no idea I possessed.

One figure spoke back to this absence of women at the heart of the form I most valued: French director Agnes Varda. Her masterly *Vagabond (San Toit, Ni Loi)* (1985) faced down the new post-political pretenders of French cinema, Carax, Luc-Besson and Beneix, with their glossy bids for the mainstream. Varda, a survivor of the macho circles of the *nouvelle vague*, offered instead a mordant account of modern Europe, charged with wintry melancholy and centring on the haunted performance of Sandrine Bonnaire. A year my junior and a riposte to the doll-women that blight French cinema, Bonnaire aged only 16 was catapulted to visibility by Maurice Pialat in *To Our Loves* (1983). At that time French cinema was producing a new wave of powerful female leads, including Isabelle Huppert, Isabel Adjani and Juliette Binoche, but Bonnaire had a raw, even stolid presence, her gaze delivering a '*fuck you*' to the camera. She seemed wounded, serious, shy; her dissent informs every frame of *Vagabond*.

Varda, a former photographer who described her style as '*cinécriture*', wrote, edited and directed the film, writing with the camera in the mode of Astruc. A former collaborator with Resnais, she dedicates her film to the great *nouveau roman* author Nathalie Sarraute, whose writing is equally suggestive in its refusal to represent reality directly. Varda '*presents*' the film in forty-seven episodes as an investigation into the death of Bonnaire's Mona. Her voice-over begins the enquiry with an elliptical offering: '*It seemed to me she came from the sea.*' Out of shot she conducts Lanzmann-like interrogations of the largely male cast who are points of reference in Mona's demise and decline. This approach instantly asserts a countering female gaze, along with a forensic relish for detail; as Varda once noted she wished to '*tell women's stories about women*'.

Vagabond is wonderfully out of sorts with the rejection of realism typifying 80s film, locating its lyricism in the Languedoc Roussillon *paysage* out of season. It's alert to the vagaries of migrant labour and the casual sexual violence that infringes on women's lives, then and now – a consciousness driving the 'Reclaim the Night' movements in Oxford who marched for bright-lit streets or picketed the notorious Private Shop around the corner from the Penultimate Picture Palace, snapping men emerging with their hoards of porn, their images displayed on lamp posts.

It's notable that the arrival of *Blue Velvet* by David Lynch in 1986 offered a litmus test around how feminism might shape our viewing, weaponised by Laura Mulvey's concept of the '*male gaze*'. We emerged aligning ourselves with or against Lynch's provocative presentation of Isabella Rossellini subjected to Denis Hopper's violent rape, an event seen voyeuristically with Kyle McLachlan's hapless Jeffrey from within the closet. The differing relationship to sexual violence of men and women, and to the act of viewing and consuming it, were laid bare here – were we watching with Jeffrey or were we watching with Dorothy? When Dorothy invites Jeffrey to visit the same violence on her as the source of her own pleasure, there was no middle ground left and walk-outs occurred.

Whatever Lynch's intentions (and other than the evasive truism of Jeffrey's question '*Why are people so bad*?' they remain obscure), the debate became a polarised one – to show or not to show. Is cinema's role to present images aligned with ideologies figuring forth a better world or to confront horror with frank representation? Does the terror of Hopper's nebulising psychopath Frank function emetically or does it legitimise what we hope it condemns? Lynch's fearless surrealism hardly makes him immune to the patriarchalism of film form; but he does at least make those deep manipulations impossible to ignore. I couldn't exempt the film from the debate it provoked, even though, from *Eraserhead* (1977) to *Inland Empire* (2006), I've gone back to Lynch's extraordinary nightmares in a state between dread and excitement.

Other critiques of film's triumphal masculinity came from within the gay artistic community, just as HIV-AIDs was about to wreak lethal havoc. Two figures embodied the excitement of this burgeoning queer cinematic tradition, Rainer Werner Fassbinder and Derek Jarman. Fassbinder died shockingly early at 37 just as I became conscious of him through his outrageous swansong, *Querelle* (1982), a swooningly erotic rendering of Jean Genet's novel (and Genet thereby became a reference point for me, driving me to stage his astonishing play *Le Balcon* (1957)). His lush artificial cinematic language animates this tale of cruising shore-leave sailors, the screen periodically bleaching out to offer monumentalised images of Genet's text. Phalluses fill every inch of the image, with underscoring throbbing below. But it was as much the headlong example of Fassbinder's wild career, retroactively politicising the glossy melodramas of Sirk and Cukor, drilling into everyday life and sexuality, that was just as exciting. Year after year, film after film, moving between raw theatre and punky film with his troubled company of actors, he flung masterpieces at the world: *Fear Eats the Soul* (1974), *Effi Brest* (1974), *Fox and His Friends,* (1975), *The Marriage of Maria Braun* (1979), *Veronika Voss* (1982). His star, the serenely beautiful and all-comprehending Hanna Schygulla, offered another riposte to my all-too male canon. Both an object of desire and an undeceived protagonist, she was his chief co-artist, complicating further his already complex male gaze. Schygulla, pals with the Baader-Meinhof Gang, fearless and defiant, exploded the place of women on the screen.

Closer to home was the fabulous work of Derek Jarman, whose route to film was through art school, punk and theatre, thereby fashioning a dazzling queer English mythology grounded in landscape, alchemy and sex. My point of entry was his version of *The Tempest* (1979). Jarman's deployment of raw film and 16 mm, suturing stock footage with the incantatory voice of Heathcote Williams, unleashing his ensemble of performers (Toyah Wilcox or the demonic Ken Campbell), startlingly fused high and low art, past and present. Revealing the camp undertow of the aesthetic of Hammer and embracing the despised theatricality of English tradition, the film defies all limiting categories of taste. To cap it all it was shot in Stoneleigh Hall in Warwickshire which I knew well. Watching it at a late-night screening I dismayed my date by being more beguiled with the film than I probably should have been with her.

Both Jarman and Fassbinder disavowed the polish and perfectionism that made the work of Kubrick and others so magnificent and yet so cold. Like chain smokers they lived through film, fashioning an overall project rather than a body of immaculate conceptions. Each film is shot through with its moment, each necessitates the next. Bertolucci once countered the backlash to his deeply flawed *Last Tango in Paris* (1972) by saying he'd taken a '*beautiful thing called politics and sullied it with a terrible thing called sex*'. Jarman and Fassbinder make that their working method, creating a canon of outsider art, indifferent to mainstream validation. Back then I paired Jarman's work with the equally quixotic, anti-narrative work of Peter Greenaway, another arts school magus. But whereas I once thrilled to *A Zed and Two Noughts* (1985) or *Drowning by Numbers* (1988), now these films seem blighted by Greenaway's icy sexual politics which reduces actors to signs and women to bodies. Jarman's work is more candid in its swooning over male bodies such as Sean Bean (*Caravaggio* (1986)) or Steven Waddington (*Edward II* (1991)); at the same time his deeply English taste for the Renaissance and Shakespeare offered a passionate counter-aesthetic.

I almost met Jarman during the brief period I was the secretary of the Oxford University Film Foundation, which I used as a chance to invite all the key figures of my filmic journey. Jarman's decorous handwriting adorned an exchange of letters as I wooed him to no avail, and I chatted to Nicolas Roeg from a telephone booth, receiving an immaculately penned decline. Greenaway did come and was as remote as his work. We dined with Ken Loach, then in a period of internal exile after Channel 4 sat on his militant work on trade unions, and hosted Alex Cox fresh from his punky success *Repo Man* (1984), or Tim Roth, hotfoot from Stephen Frears's sly thriller *The Hit* (1985).

But more significantly the Film Foundation was a hub for would-be film-makers. We'd come a year after the startling success of *Privileged*, Oxford American student

Michael Hoffman's debut which launched Hugh Grant and Imogen Stubbs as Sloaney actors staging *The Duchess of Malfi* (an idea nicked from Jacques Rivette's *Paris Nous Appartient* (1961)). It traded in all the clichés of Oxford that could be trafficked in and we'd decided to hate it; but we struggled to make our answer to it.

One of our core members was a likeable public schoolboy, Justin Hardy, son of the director of the cult masterpiece *The Wicker Man* (1973), Robin Hardy. Hardy Jnr and my American friend Mike Hasselmo, a psychologist, hammered out a script for a short, unenticingly entitled *First and Final*, its theme a stressed Oxford student having a breakdown during his final exams. So much for banishing the ghost of *Privileged*! But in an astonishing coup, Hardy tempted Polish cinematographer Andrezj Sekula to shoot it, a sardonic creative force who quickly clocked he was working with a bunch of amateurs and then went on to film *Reservoir Dogs* and *Pulp Fiction*. Strangely enough we don't appear on his IMDB page.

I was location scout and boom handler. The experience of making the film was fun and tedious in equal measure as we waited for Andrezj to get the right light, got in the way of colleges in the conference season and realised how tough it is to make a film of any quality whatsoever. We went on to make even quirkier film *The Gravyman*, based on an Ivor Cutler poem and shot largely in the exciting dusty sinister galleries of the Pitt Rivers anthropological museum.

I can't make great claims for my sound design but I did find myself gripped by the role of sound in film storytelling, not simply the accompaniment of the image, but a place of choice and emphasis. The heightened sound of water in Tarkovsky; the weird dubbing in Pasolini which make utterance a kind of violence; the repeated sound gestures in Bresson which form a kind of punctuation.

Yet in truth I was more excited by theatre-making; here technology was less central to the task – the intractably segmented, even logistical focus of film bored me even as the result thrilled me. Everything was subordinated to the demands of the camera, the boom mike, the slow edit. And the world of film seemed so far away whereas the realm of theatre felt close to hand, one dependent on capital, the other simply on will. As my peers went off to film school or worked as runners on sets, I knew whatever my route to the screen was, it would be an indirect one.

Act Two Living

(BRISTOL)

EXT. WATERFRONT, BRISTOL. NIGHT.
Filthy water slops against the floating dock;
shrubs shroud wharves, roofless warehouses lie
exposed to the sky; irregular streets of Georgian
houses rise to the arc of Brunel's suspension
bridge.

The end of the 80s was a sour pay-off for the triumphalism of what Stuart Hall first dubbed 'Thatcherism'. If there was hope in a country frogmarched into post-industrialism, it was to be found in regional cities reinventing themselves, cities such as my new home – Bristol.

With the collapse of manufacturing, the fortunes of dad's employer Rolls Royce waned. In 1985 he was redeployed to their Filton works north of the city; we moved to follow him. As the virus of neoliberalism pulsed through the economy, Margaret Thatcher's dogma of privatisation ensured that the aero division dad worked for was thrown onto the cold market again in 1987.

Shifting workplace is never easy, but dad's new role was repugnant to him. As the enforcer of lay-offs, sackings and redundancies, he was now officially the class enemy. Bristolian working culture had at its heart a tight-knit, rebellious trade unionism, that in the past had produced the legendary Ernest Bevin. The daily aggro in his new plant might have been bearable if he'd been backed by those above him, but his bosses flinched at any risk of strike action. He was pincered between shop floor and boardroom – then, deemed surplus to requirements, took redundancy as the 90s began.

The Norman Tebbit injunction that the jobless had to '*get on (their) bike(s)*' to re-enter the labour market has little value for a man in his fifties. Dad tried out a dizzying variety of careers, posing as an iced-yoghurt salesman ('*I can't believe it's yoghurt!*') or a stint reparking cars for hotel guests. He took it on the chin; there was no room for critiquing the system – as Barbara Ehrenreich has written, it was *Smile or Die* (2009) – and he'd often rebuked me for my '*negative intelligence*'. As nothing stuck, he threw his dwindling pay-off into an ailing workshop where, on a battered lathe, he refashioned machine tool parts for bakeries and engineers, finally his own master.

Mum had left one low-paid job for a patchwork of volunteering while fielding her mother's death, husband's lay-off and my sister's divorce. With typical chutzpah she skilled up, taking on a chiropody practice, spending her days driving from care home to care home, lap covered with a towel ready to receive the feet of the old and infirm. Alan Bennett displayed exquisite timing by penning his hymn to chiropody, with Michael Palin tending to the inherently comic feet of others in *A Private Function* (1984).

She found herself halted in her tracks, bursting into unbidden tears, slow to rise in the morning, unable to sleep at night. Mental illness was unmentionable to us, but mum was floored by an overdue depression, in mourning for her life.

Living in a new city none of us could claim didn't help. My parents' relentless sociality yielded invites, not least as stalwarts of the local Rotary set. But how deep did the new friendships go? After all the days on the golf course and the safari suppers, the fun runs and sponsored walks, there was little appetite for confessions of loss. Nonetheless, slowly, surely, Bristol saved them, opened up a new passion for where they lived; something I grew to share.

Our first house was in a 70s estate cresting the rise of the town of Portishead; its dormer windows looked north over the Bristol Channel into the coastal plain of South Wales, and, on clear days, the gathered blue peaks of the Brecon Beacons. The channel granted an epic scope to things, the drama of weather measured out by the slow progress of container ships. The Severn, puckered by variegated currents, turbid and brown, gathered Panavision skies and startling sunsets into its waters.

Portishead was synonymous with the eponymous trip-hop band who, with Massive Attack, emerged at that time, although its figurehead Geoff Barrow described it as '*a place people go to die*'. It's a commuter town sprawled over the Gordano Valley, humped against the mild humours of the channel; its coastal paths dip and rise over shingly coves with burnt-out fires, hemmed in by caravan parks or golf courses.

I knew no one here. I exchanged busy Oxford for this blank slate, claiming the dole and walking the dog along the tideline wishing I was elsewhere. University positions you in a whirlwind of networks which prove illusory on exit. And what was my life to be grounded in? Writing? Being a film director? What was my work and place in that elusive thing, the economy?

We moved closer into Bristol, to Pill, a community of ex-stevedores now beached in social housing on a bend in the Avon as it coils its way through steep gorges towards the city. Despite the city being 4 miles away, the village felt confounded in the downs, hedged in by woodland and great estates. But I could cycle in along the river path where kiln workings and rail tracks filleted stands of hanging trees, winding up to Brunel's suspension bridge, a dramatic portal into the city, where I freewheeled from Clifton's Georgian heights to the neglected docks.

Bristol, now a crucible of decolonisation and site of the astonishing coup of Black Lives Matter protestors dethroning the statue of slave trader Edward Coulson, was then starting its long exit from industrialism and maritime history. It sought to reinvent itself as the capital of the West, incubating ecologically minded downshifters alongside a resurgent financial sector and that familiar pathway to regeneration, culture.

Buzzing with music and clubs, and the birthplace of the man who went on to be Cary Grant, Archie Leach, Bristol has been surprisingly absent from film. Other than the short-lived delights of the 1979 TV cop show *Shoestring,* its seductive 'jazzy' theme following the young Trevor Eve descending the Christmas Steps and pushing faders in his Radio West studio, the only cinematic portrait is Chris Petit's haunting road movie *Radio On* (1979). The film tracks a DJ's journey from London along the M4 to discern the fate of his brother. Its debt to New German cinema is made explicit with the presence of Lisa Kreuzer, a Kraftwerk soundtrack and Wenders's cinematographer Martin Schafer who shot the seminal road movies *Alice in the Cities* (1974) and *Kings of the Road* (1976). In Petit's monochrome gaze Bristol is a web of flyovers and dank wharves, like an even more down-at-heel Hamburg.

But this city was where I learned how to negotiate the make-work that capitalism finds for us. I'd had jobs since my teens, rarely requiring skill. I'd flipped eggs in a local services for tired truckers; I signed up to agency bussing in temps to undercut toy workers in a Swindon factory; I'd walked insurance files from floor to floor; I'd been lectured by young managers seated under posters proclaiming '*The Customer is King*'. The diktat that work will make you free was hard to argue with in Thatcher's utopia of unfettered entrepreneurialism; as a graduate of English Lit, I had surprisingly little to bring to the party.

I found more agreeable work at a bookshop, *Georges*, at the top of Park Street as it falls away steeply from the Wills Memorial Building; at least I liked books. I worked in goods inward, unpacking boxes hauled up from deliveries in the tiny lifts to the fourth floor, a cockpit over the city; then wheeling blue tubs of them to their destination in their different classifications. How many pointless books there seemed in the world, as I ripped open box after box, their glossy covers beaming out the forlorn hope of being sold. Eventually I'd lug a good proportion of them back to be remaindered. If I had any illusions about publishing, they died during that job; books seemed to be just one more commodity.

But work creates other pleasures – watching how life-long workers maintain their spirits was one. Up in the stockroom was the hilariously sardonic Bristolian Bob, hardly as high as the workbench, face lost in thick specs, merrily spouting scorn, filth and profanity in a lispy Bris'l lilt. His wordless audience of some decades was the mournful Colin, tall, fifty-something, unmarried, an afficionado of bossa nova, smiling away Bob's incessant venting. I'd raise the shutter of the loading bay to paid-up Communist Party activist Tony hymning the future of the USSR just as it was disintegrating.

My saviour was a lanky guy in Politics, Phil from Westbury-on-Trym, smuggling out knocked off copies of Tom Nairn and Edward Said. Phil was a skilled practitioner of situationism. He sidled up to me to invite me to join him on *derivements*, surrealist traverses of the city inspired by Guy Debord's *The Society of the Spectacle* (1967); we used '*aleatory*' techniques of chance to render Bristol a living board game. One day he announced we were to visit every road in the A-Z called 'West Road' – turned out there were quite a few. On arrival at the first West Road, he announced we were to advance along the road taking photographs at 10-foot intervals. I solemnly performed my allotted task, ignoring the puzzled indulgent gazes of passers-by.

I shifted to a caring job at a residential home. Leigh Court was a Palladian mansion in Bath stone set in grounds designed by Repton, doubtless built on slaving money. Here living in wilful isolation was a community of young adults with severe learning disabilities, following the underexamined tenets of theosophist Rudolf Steiner. I was brought in untrained to oversee residents during their troubled nights, awoken by bed-wetting, displays of guileless sexuality, or violent frustration – one scary night I found myself waiting out a fit of fury by one lad wrenching a sink from its fixings, feeling a little like Shelley Duvall cowering from Jack Nicholson on the rampage in *The Shining*. My mournful shifts were full of broken sleep and the sudden terrifying convulsions of epilepsy, and I was poorly equipped to meet the complex needs of my charges.

A lad called Robert, who never spoke and had at all times to make contact with any wall or door to hand, grew close to me, his face lit up by a serene, confused smile. I'd walk him to bed with aching slowness as he fumbled his way along the corridor. On one shift a taxi pulled up admitting a man with a skinhead cut; given we were a mile from the road, this was pretty troubling. He stood angrily ringing our bell; inside I was in lone charge of my twelve clients for the night. I gingerly answered the door. The skinhead shouted he was Robert's brother, that he'd come to take his brother home, and barged his way in bristling for a fight, '*Where is he, where fucking is he*?' Robert, hovering on the stairs, looked as scared as me. My threat of the police seemed to quickly puncture the tattooed Irish brother's rescue bid; he crumpled, confessed to having been 'sectioned' himself, that he'd walked free unchallenged from his institution to find Robert, all he had by way of family. With some regret I booked him another cab and he left, crushed, to no clear fate.

Yet, in the spirit of my mother, and maybe of my own past, I found myself at home in this battered elegant house, beloved by that guileless community. We took rhapsodic walks into the grounds, or minibus trips to Weston-super-Mare, innocents all, as if in a Fellini film. This was real work, rooted in care and necessity and protected from money; here I had to get out of my own head, found myself loved and needed.

But I needed skills – after all, I wanted a career in the 'Creative Industries'. I wrote to TV companies, film production companies, jazz touring agencies, all to no avail. With a nation of the young warehoused on unemployment benefit, the government finagled training opportunities galore, the names of initiatives constantly changing: YOP, YTS, MSC, gateways into entrepreneurial futures which rarely arrived. I volunteered for an 'Action Line' phone-in that accompanied the broadcasts of BBC Radio Bristol, assembling support packs ('*If you or your family have been affected by any of the issues in this programme . . .*') or splicing together interviews with union reps or a professor of Industrial Relations at Bristol University who characterised workplace injuries as a hidden wounds of capitalism. I walked the city with a reel-to-reel like Geraldine Chaplin in Robert Altman's *Nashville* (1975) and began to see myself as a citizen of Bristol, decoding its complex geography and history, a product of power and capital. And here again cinemas were my guide.

Bristol was graced with two innovative venues located in the abandoned docks, on Canons Marsh and the facing Narrow Quay; the former, Watershed, was a focal point for film-making and viewing; the latter, the Arnolfini, was a gallery and cinema in an old tea warehouse. The Watershed opened in 1982 and looked like the future; its three screens filtered a world of radical and innovative film-making, as well as providing training and workshops for would-be artists. Both institutions were beacons in the transformation of the floating harbour into that classic 80s fulcrum of gentrification, the waterfront.

This Bristol coincided with my deepening sense of film's political power, as a form of resistance to High Thatcherism, an insight sharpened by my reading of *Marxism Today* or *New Left Review*. And this notion was exemplified by the films of Jean-Luc Godard. I'd binged on another late-night Channel 4 season which focused on his reviled late 'political' films after he repudiated conventional cinema in 1968. Colin McCabe and Laura Mulvey's crucial primer *Godard: Images Sounds Politics* (1980), which I bought in huge excitement from the Arnolfini bookshop, was my guide to films such as *Le Gai Savoir* (1969), *Tout Va Bien* (1972), *Numero Deux* (1975). These experiments interrogated film's form, social function and the workings of everyday life, by means of a strange fusion of Marx, Mao and early Soviet director Dziga-Vertov. Later I'd work backwards to early Godard and come to understand him as stylist as much as ideologue, come to love the formal and experiential adventure of his 60s work – the stark simple Brechtian images of *Le Petit Soldat* (1963) or *Vivre Sa Vie* (1962); the wild Matisse-like colours of *Le Mépris* (1963) or *Pierrot Le Fou* (1965). But it was his late and unloved films that spoke most clearly to me in my new predicament.

The austerity of these acts of auto-interrogation felt like the ideal soundtrack to my life in the shallows of capitalism. Take the impenetrably boring but fascinating *Numero Deux*. It offers a steady blank gaze at the economics of film production, with Godard noting of himself, '*I am the boss and also the worker.*' This critique is set against a split-screen account of the bleak lives of a middle-class couple, and not least the anality of their sex life. The 'film' collapses essay and documentary, paying little heed to the viewer or narrative – as David Thomson protested, it's part of a vein of Godard's work that is '*pathological and humourless*'. Yet Godard's refusal of both the capitalist underpinnings of cinema itself as well as the world beyond it spoke to me in that moment. Even more affecting was *Tout Va Bien*, which tracks a strike at a sausage factory, with the incongruous presence of 'stars' Yves Montand and Jane Fonda, merely two more signs in the film's semiotic system. The Brecht-like tableaux of factories with their fourth wall removed like stage sets, the direct address to camera of Fonda and Montand, the sudden jump-cuts and interruption of placards as *v-effekts* and then the final brilliant tracking shop along the tills of a supermarket as riot police lay into protesters combined to make the film bracingly confrontational in its depiction of capitalism as crisis.

Godard's revision of Brecht offered an aesthetic of interruption matched by an unapologetically cerebral approach to form. And I needed film as a tool to analyse the life that I found myself in, to analyse the fate of my family and the future of the country.

I was moved to throw myself into whatever I understood communism to be, seeking out the offices of the 'Communist Party of Bristol, Bath and Gloucester' (possibly the least revolutionary movement imaginable?) located in a side street of the Old Market area. The very nice woman who greeted me there couldn't find the appropriate membership form to enable me, as Lukacs had said, to get my 'entry ticket into history'. The Communist Party of Great Britain (CPGB) was a meagre endeavour in 1988, split between its Leninist rump and the more progressive version that identified with Euro-Communism. In the few meetings I attended the best it could seem to hope for would be to a fist fight with members of the local National Front. Nonetheless I did a sponsored cycle to Cardiff to support of striking dock workers and this flirtation with communism informed my travels to Hungary, Czechoslovakia and Yugoslavia just as each was venturing into their own versions of the glasnost-style liberalisation being unleashed in the USSR. That thaw was marked in Bristol by the opening of a bistro called 'Perestroika'. The possibility of what writer Anthony Barnett optimistically dubbed Soviet Freedom (1988) was in the air; without irony I eagerly obtained his excitable book from Full Marx, a bookshop on the Cheltenham Road.

There was a more nuanced cinema of political change in the wake of Godard that resisted his puritanism, and the Watershed was its home. Take the films of the Black Audio Film Collective and especially of Ghanaian-born director and artist John Akomfrah. His haunting short Handsworth Sounds (1986) filtered the supple thinking of Stuart Hall into an angry yet lyrical film-essay about the Birmingham riots of 1981, dub reggae layered over images of tabloid racist vitriol and the brutal overreaction of the police. Akomfrah paved the way for the work of the great Steve McQueen also positioned between the gallery and the big screen and it's fitting that years later I saw Akomfrah's stunning installations tracking the legacy of colonialism, Tropika (2016) and Auto-da-Fe (2016), at the Arnolfini. Equally exciting were the queer-eyed investigations of Isaac Julien whose elegant Looking for Langston (1989) asserted a lineage of gay-black identity with the Harlem Renaissance's patron saint Langston Hughes and whose Young Soul Rebels (1991) offered a lush revisitation of the punk moment through the eyes of two gay Afro-Caribbean men. Films like these set out to rethink the nation, invested with the multicultural energy that first surfaced in Hanif Kureishi and Stephen Frears's My Beautiful Laundrette (1985). But most revelatory to me was the work of Scottish director Bill Douglas and his masterly Comrades (1986).

I'd seen the small canon of Douglas's films eked out through the 70s thanks to the tireless patronage of British Film Institute (BFI) Head of Production Mamoun Hassan. His bleak, compacted autobiographical trilogy – My Childhood (1972), My Ain Folk (1973), My Way Home (1978) – sculpted in Gale Tattersall's stark, woodcut-like images offered a poetic reading of Scottish poverty, fusing the lyrical neo-realism of directors such as Satyajit Ray with the visual rigour of Pudovkin. Douglas spent most of the 80s battling to fund his epic about the Tolpuddle martyrs, the Dorset pioneers of trade unionism transported to Australia for their temerity in forming a union or 'Combination'.

His project was a very 70s one, paralleling the radical 'History from Below' movement evident in the work of E. P. Thompson, Christopher Hill and Sheila Rowbotham; or the criticism of Raymond Williams whose essay 'Culture is Ordinary' (1958) inverted my sense of where to locate cultural value. Hassan was also responsible for promoting the production of the work of film historian Kevin Brownlow whose lost masterpiece *Winstanley* (1975) offers another startlingly vivid reconstruction of the life of the radical leader of the Levellers movement during the English Civil War.

The slow genesis of Douglas's film brought it into a very different world, as history reverted to the task of heritage, a shift analysed by Raphael Samuel in *Theatres of Memory* (1994) or Patrick Wright's *On Living in an Old Country* (1985), and epitomised by the elegant, airy films of Merchant-Ivory – although ironically James Ivory had been a key producer for Douglas. History from above was back and *Comrades'* contrarian sense of the past was robbed of the acclaim it merited. Yet for me it was a revelation not least because it gathered together all the cultural landscapes of my life, fashioning images on a painterly scale that could only be compared to Bergman. Scenes of rural drudgery in Paul Nash fieldscapes, the workers in sodden garments glimpsing their masters in the lit-up advent calendar of the manor, unlocked my childhood in Long Lawford for inspection. The rural squalor filmed in the abandoned village of Tyneham, the counterintuitive casting of the cream of British theatre in cameos as landowners (Vanessa Redgrave, Freddie Jones, Robert Stephens) with the martyrs in the foreground played by then largely unknown performers (but soon to be knowns: Phil Davies, Imelda Staunton, Keith Allen) placed the people i'd grown up with at the centre of the narrative. The performance of Robin Soans as their leader George Loveless embodied this luminous simplicity without condescension or sentiment (Robin would later be the magnificent centre of my plays *The Contingency Plan* (2009)). Equally it was not parochial, with the shock of the martyrs' transposition to the arid ochre colours of Australia delivered with the terseness of Bunuel.

Douglas wrote screenplays like a poet, leaving out as much as he articulated and insinuating the meaning of the action through what Eisenstein called '*the third sense*' of montage. Yet central to the appeal of his film is its theatricality; having worked with Joan Littlewood's ensemble, Douglas had imbibed Brechtian storytelling, of tableaux, juxtaposition and stylisation. For all the gorgeous realism of the film, it is informed by a strand of self-reflection, embodied in the presence of actor Alex Norton, avatar of the radical Scottish theatre company *7:84*, who plays thirteen roles: the bearer of the magic lantern, the diorama or the silhouette, all cinema's precursors. *Comrades* gathered all the forces at work on me – a resistance to capitalism and the compulsion of work, a desire for radical art, a wish for a history that spoke to my own experience – and burned itself into my heart. What was shocking was how little impact it had at the time, proving at best a *succès d'estime*. Douglas died of cancer in 1991; his struggles to create a radical British cinema testified to the inhospitable climate for radical film in this country.

I had to change tack; maybe my route to film was to be writing, filtering the inchoate experiences of my new life. I applied to film schools on the back of my strange allegorical screenplay *Reflections from a Damaged City*, its pompous title nodding to Adorno's subtitle for *Minima Moralia* (1951), its content a confused mash-up of Jarman, Godard, Coventry, my father, pretty much everything I was reading and seeing. It had a poetic rather than a narrative logic; it barely acknowledged character; it eschewed naturalism. Needless to say it didn't do the trick.

But I knew whatever I did next I wanted it to count – so I applied to train to be a teacher.

(OXFORD)

INT. CLASSROOM, OXFORDSHIRE COMPREHENSIVE. MORNING.
A scrubby schoolroom with chalk-smeared board. A
class of indifferent yet quiescent kids in green
uniforms; a MAN IN DULL-BROWN SUIT moves among
them as they run their fingers over the pages of a
class reader. TWO TRAINEE TEACHERS sit at one
remove.

There's few things scarier than going back to school – as a teacher.

Stepping in front of the class is like stepping onstage with the house lights up and the audience there under duress. Doing so in an Oxfordshire comprehensive where the kids owe you nothing is a fine corrective to any would-be Oxbridge Marxist writer.

It looked easy enough; my fellow trainee teacher Claire and I had been observing the downbeat lessons of our mentor John with fourth-year bottom set English for a few weeks. As we commuted home, I'd slate what I saw as the dull teaching of dull books – Priestley's *An Inspector Calls* (1945) for fuck's sake! In 1989! John certainly made few claims for his own teaching; he didn't have high hopes for what was possible in this comprehensive school in Witney, a small town 12 miles from Oxford, later to be David Cameron's constituency. The kids were children of rural labourers, farmers and builders; they could have been my peers in Long Lawford. Wasn't this a chance to unleash intellectual shock rather than manage low expectations? I'd got where I was by a series of ruptures; time to provide one for them.

The day came when John dared to leave us alone with the class. There was a thrill in the room as I stood in front of them, opening Walt Whitman's *Leaves of Grass* (1855) to read 'Song of Myself' – this would throw the switch on the tracks of the mediocre educational parochialism condemning the students to what Bevin once called '*the poverty of their desires*'. Of course, I wasn't fooled by the sentiment of Robin Williams's strategy in Peter Weir's *Dead Poets Society* (1989) even if this was straight from his playbook; I was driven by the vision of the classroom as a utopian space such as that shown in Godard's stark parable *Le Gai Savoir* – the joy of knowledge indeed!

The class granted us a honeymoon of about 10 minutes' puzzled attention, punctuated by the odd volley of giggling; we moved among them, breaking apart hierarchies of space, challenging Marxist Louis Althusser's description of the school as 'Ideological State Apparatus'. The noise level began to rise, as we tended to a student here, a student there, this rising wave becoming harder to stem with our genial ssshhing. But in the midst of the furore was the clear sound of dissent from a sour-eyed lad called Kevin who John had warned us about.

No, Kevin didn't go in for this wanky American poem, Kevin didn't want to write some stupid 'song of myself' and he told us as much in full voice, kicking back the desk and rocking on his chair. The class fell into an appalled hush – 'Honestly I don't know what the fuck you want me to do' –that word, barely heard in a classroom in a school back then, pitched the possibility of transgression about as high as could be imagined. The kids gleefully swerved their heads as one to me: how would the weird student teacher who looked like Egon from *Ghostbusters* (1984) handle this one?

I had nothing to offer; Claire stood horrified at the back of the room. I found myself blurting, 'You do not say "fuck" in my lesson' compounding Kevin's felony and raising the ante all at once. Oh, the class was delighted, this was turning out to be a hell of a lesson. Now Kevin was up and out of his chair and out of the room, his finest provocation yet – what now Egon? Claire shrugged helplessly. I could only give chase, with no idea where this would lead; I bolted out into the corridor, ran with little dignity after him, swerved in his path and pinned him to a wall.

A smile of triumph ignited Kevin's face – so was I really going to dare to, what, hit him? Was I really holding the lapels of his blazer? Was I not aware corporal punishment was actually now illegal? Or maybe I was some sort of child abuser? I had no idea what to do next – I stepped back and he was gone, out of there, aloft on his triumph. Kevin was the teacher and it was I who'd learned his lesson.

But what *had* I learned? Like all traumas, and this was one, the lesson would take time to land but it was like the first encounter with a sceptical theatre audience, with a pack of critics, with a public you dare to speak to who have no idea why you assume you should. And there were other lessons that year equally shocking to a young communist joining the party just as it was winding up. That autumn of 1989 saw the fall of the Berlin Wall and the revelation that whatever 'Actually Existing Socialism' had been it hadn't rested on the popular will. That rash of bloodless revolutions in countries I had been celebrating in their final year of autocracy created a real cognitive challenge – would I stand with the besieged, discredited figures of Egon Krenz or Janos Kadar or Gustav Husak or the excited jubilant crowds pushing their statues off podia? The glint in Margaret Thatcher's eye or the benign smile of George H. W. Bush hardly helped me pick the right side. But I didn't renew my Communist Party membership.

The decision to return to Oxford to take up a PGCE had been a leap into what I thought of as praxis, genuine political and cultural action in the classroom. This was a period of crackdown as Tory education secretary Kenneth Baker curbed the perceived radicalism of the education sector, exemplified by the unapologetically multicultural Inner London Education Authority (ILEA). Baker's secret weapon was the National Curriculum, a standardising assault on what Jim Callaghan had called the 'secret gardens' of the teacher's classroom autonomy. In the Department of Education at

Norham Gardens in leafy Summertown, these moves met with stout resistance. A bunch of us left-leaning teachers headed up by a wickedly funny Glaswegian called Mac Daly (later the author of *A Primer in Marxist Aesthetics*) weighed in, on the one hand turning on the slack liberal humanist values (*'liberal'* and *'humanist'* being dirty words back then) while in an act of contortion, seeking to defend schools from illiberal and not especially humanist Tory onslaughts. Although we were training as teachers of English we were more gripped by the idea of Media and Cultural Studies in the tradition of Raymond Williams, embodied in our lecturer, Chris, an amiable fellow film buff who once proudly removed a book by right-wing educationalist Rhodes Boyson from the library as a form of direct action. I found myself learning rather more immediately useful stuff from former teacher Hazel, fresh from the classroom.

My English lessons were generally a chance to proselytise for film; I'd bring in worn-out VHS cassettes pirated from television to analyse sequences from anything I could get away with. I'd teach James Vance Marshall's rather slight novel *Walkabout* (1959) so I could screen the astonishing opening of Roeg's film and Edward Bond's screenplay, with its haunting audit of the strangeness of Australia, jump-cutting from Jenny Agutter's voice lessons to her mother chopping up kangaroo meat above a Hockneyesque swimming pool to her father blowing his brains out in a VW beetle in the outback. To illustrate a lesson in genre I would unsheathe Godard's *Alphaville* (1965) where film noir, sci-fi and Brechtian documentary rub shoulders.

I was now back in an Oxford obscured from me as an undergraduate, an Oxford of council estates off the Cowley Road, or rural satellite towns and villages, harbouring hidden poverty – Witney, Thame, Wheatley. Here middle-class kids were creamed off into independent schools leaving complex communities of what were euphemistically called *'mixed abilities'*. But for all the catastrophic beginnings of my teaching career, I began to relish the classroom as a place to experiment in participatory democracy even if I was bound to experience regular and dismaying failure.

My first job was in Lord Williams's School in Thame, an amalgam of an old grammar recognisable to me from Sheriff and a secondary modern, whose split site reflected those separate histories. I was hired as a teacher of English and Drama. The English was a stretch but the Drama was entirely outside my comfort zone. The skeptical Head of Drama, a former actor, Val, felt aggrieved that I'd been imposed on her simply because the headteacher had enjoyed my performance as Danny Zuko in a production of *Grease* (1978) at his wife's school. If that was true, it was an odd audition for the job, given it involved me snogging the sixth former playing Sandy night after night. It wouldn't get past the police now, let alone Ofsted.

Yes, Val had a point. I had written on Brecht and acquired a theoretical interest in him but had no experience in Drama and would have to learn on the job. That was tough on my first GCSE group who, in having me as their teacher, felt they'd drawn the short straw. My first lesson only confirmed that feeling - I threw an extract from Peter Handke's radical so-called '*Sprechstucke*', *Offending the Audience* (1966) at twenty puzzled 14-year-olds and sat back while they rose to the challenge of shrieking, shouting and abusing each other; an hour later three tearful students defected to Val's group. Well, I salute those who stayed with me – for we were all embarked on an adventure where the avant-garde collided with the reality of students needing to pass exams. As for Handke, now the controversial recipient of the Nobel Prize for Literature in 2019 and notorious for his defence of Serbian ethnic cleanser Slobodan Milosevic, back then he was the exciting collaborator of Wim Wenders who adapted his brilliant slim existentialist novel *The Goalie's Anxiety at the Penalty Kick* in 1972, and directed his visionary account of Berlin as viewed by angels, *Wings of Desire* (1987). Handke occupied the sweet spot between literature, theatre and film. But he was a world away from Oxfordshire Drama students habituated to jolly impro games and well-meaning devising.

Nonetheless teaching Drama was my second education, which took off when my new Head of Drama, Simon, permitted me to take on Theatre Studies. I had to learn about Stanislavski, Antonin Artaud, Edward Gordon Craig and of course Bertolt Brecht, diving in so deeply that my filmic education fell away. We drove the school minibus to see theatre as I had never seen it before; Berkoff, Théâtre de Complicité, Neil Bartlett, Pete Brooks, Forced Entertainment. We rarely saw plays; the fashion was for physical theatre, informed by Artaud's dream of a *Theatre of Cruelty*, all bold design and choreographed movement. Plays were out of date, naturalism dead in the ditch. Graduates of Jacques Lecoq's school in Paris where mime was the order of the day predominated and the verbal was treated with deep suspicion. This anti-literary ethos fused with a residual prejudice against 'text' in classroom Drama, dismissed as elitist and divisive.

Yet I was directing – and writing. After all I had a captive theatre company in my students, avid to perform, many of them girls, with too few roles to draw on. To feed that hunger I penned a sprawling account of Victorian life for my lower school kids, peppered with ideas drawn directly from *Comrades* and Brecht. *Tales from a Stereopticon* patched together Mayhew's accounts of urban poverty with bits of Dicken and Blake, building to a critique of imperialism which backfired as the cast of 13-year-olds sardonically launched into 'Rule Britannia' only to find the audience joining in with none of the appropriate irony. To mark the signing of the Maastricht Treaty in 1992 I directed Buchner's *Woyzeck* (1836), a play I'd acquired an unhealthy obsession with, inspired by Herzog's somnambulist version of it in 1979. I plundered the ideas of David Lynch, ending my production of Steven Berkoff's version of Kafka's *Metamorphosis* (1969) with Roy Orbison.

To be alive and a Drama teacher in those end-days of Thatcherism was in Wordsworth's words '*a very heaven*'. After my faltering start, the students were up for anything and I was among passionate colleagues under the tenure of a head teacher who was a model of liberalism. We had a scruffy black-box drama studio, we had talented young actors for free (many of whom went on to successful theatre careers), we could programme what we liked, experiment with light, costume, music as if we were the auteurs we taught and studied. And they paid me for this!

The early 90s were, in retrospect, at times a confused, euphoric period; it was forgivable of American diplomat Francis Fukuyama to proclaim we were entering '*the end of history*'. I was called out on my residual commitment to socialism by my friend Stephen who, on entering the civil service, announced that politics from now on was about *'liberal democracy'*. Yet the Conservatives were still in power and I was frantically running off some hand-outs at the photocopier when a colleague sidled up to me to reveal that Margaret Thatcher had stepped down. This felt momentous – but only complicated the task of opposition.

Well I had other things to think about –falling in love for one. And one of the sites where that love was found and fixed was in the dark of the cinema.

I didn't always make the right call. I ruined one date by imagining Bergman's terrifying fable of rape and revenge *The Virgin Spring* (1960) might make for a romantic watch. I then made matters worse by suggesting Robert Altman's *McCabe and Mrs Miller* (1971) might atone for my faux pas, with its wintry Klondike setting and Julie Christie as brothel-owner; my date left in the first reel. My prime venue for arcane date nights was Rewley House, a former convent tucked off St Giles, and the hub for the Oxford University Department for Continuing Education. Here in a raked lecture hall we'd head on Sunday nights to see film scholars such as Mike Weaver and Sarah Street compere obscure screenings at a time when Oxford formally disavowed Film Studies. And one particular delight in 1990 was *The White Hell of Pitz Palu* (1929), a silent black-and-white mountain adventure directed by Arnold Fanck and G. W. Pabst known to me because of his film of Brecht's *Threepenny Opera*.

My guest on this night was PhD student and feminist scholar Hero Chalmers – later to become my wife. Friends had engineered a friendship between us, but romance seemed unlikely. I was very keen to impress Hero who was remarkable for her exotic name and the length of her chestnut hair, a fiercely intelligent woman onto whom I projected an unhelpful patina of feminist seriousness. This had, on one occasion, led to a misunderstanding. I'd been hotly rehearsing my radfem credentials by declaring my Andrea Dworkin-inspired loathing of pornography, singling out the magazine *Hustler* for particularly damning comment. This, confusingly, prompted an oddly liberal reaction from Hero; in fact she seemed quite relaxed with *Hustler*, claiming she'd enjoyed it a great deal. Baffled, I nodded, gazed at my pint, a bit non-plussed; so maybe I'd taken the wrong tack. Maybe Hero was one of those elusive libertarian post-feminists, a Camille Paglia say. Time perhaps for a reset? Only later did it emerge that she'd been referring to Robert Rossen's 1961 movie *The Hustler*, which featured a lithe Paul Newman crouched intent over the pool table and, on its revival, launched a passion for the pursuit in impressionable middle-class hipsters.

So perhaps a rare screening of one of the pinnacles of expressionist cinema might make amends for that false start? Hero was at Brasenose College, in the difficult foothills of her PhD which pioneered scholarship into Early Modern women writers such as Margaret Cavendish and Aphra Behn. Intellectually she was the real deal, an Oxford scholar; whereas I was some rookie teacher mugging up on my subject day to day with no particular direction in life.

On arrival at Rewley House it became apparent this film was going to be no easy view – the scholarly crib sheet on our seat revealed the film was just shy of three hours long. Mmm. Three hours of a silent movie; that could be a very long three hours. And had I made that sufficiently clear? The next bombshell was that its female star was none other than the dazzling Aryan fascist Leni Riefenstahl. Would Hero think I thought that was OK? That maybe here I was, some sort of neo-Nazi getting off on Hitler's squeeze, this cold blonde propagandist-in-chief of the Nuremberg Rally, jumping crevasses and brandishing an ice pick for three endless silent hours? The film began, oscillating between picture-postcard peaks and shaky intertext. My God, this was going to be an arduous 160 minutes. Hero was close to, but we weren't anywhere near a state in which I might venture an exploratory hand onto her knee or the like – and anyway what a vulgar objectifying thought to be having about a feminist scholar! What did I think this was, an out-take from Barry Levinson's 1982 buddy movie *Diner*?

More mountains, Christ, and we're only an hour in; and the soundtrack's an endless thrashing about of sub-Wagnerian motifs. She's awake at least, turning to smile at me. But isn't there something deeply unerotic about the *Bergfilme* genre, all those cold heights and that tedious muscular striving? What kind of signal did I think I was sending? And naturally there's no intermission at Rewley House, education not pleasure is the order of the day. Certainly no ice creams and we're a way from the pub. Maybe The Eagle and Child? But we won't be out of here till 11 and I'm teaching at 9.

Oh yes it was a long film and in truth often a tedious one, distant actors crawling across snowfields, and with the old print, what seemed to be snow was often mere scratches on celluloid. And in the amateur scholarly cave of the Rewley House projection frequently gave way to white screens, ending the show abruptly with the scattered attendees trapped into an awkward post-screen analysis. But I thank it for filling up Sunday nights before the working week commenced with pretexts to lure Hero away from her research.

Film has been a long shared but complicated pleasure for us. I see her as a kind of ethical bellwether, able to call out specious arguments for the representation of women, the glib introduction of violence or cheap transgression. We moved in together; then to the horror of our flatmate, later to become a Brexiteer journalist, things changed. Again, film played a part; I'd been to Bristol to see my parents, lamenting the lack of love in my life and meeting up with an ex before seeing Scorsese's latest, *Goodfellas* (1990), for me his last great film, hectic, shocking, funny and headlong. By the time I returned to Oxford, Hero saw me differently and I realised where my future lay. A film changed my life that night.

And while teaching had its pleasures I was on a treadmill of work and marking and no closer to writing, despite some odd little screenplays which drew a surprisingly warm response from Channel 4. I wrote my first full-length screenplay, *The Student of Clouds*, a lyrical if clichéd account of a teacher trying to rescue a student from abuse. Maybe I wasn't entirely misguided in my hopes; perhaps more study would help?

I applied to the University of East Anglia (UEA), but I was no novelist; I applied to various courses in directing; and I applied to a new course in playwriting at the University of Birmingham run by someone I'd at least heard of, David Edgar.

Here I was to have more luck.

(BIRMINGHAM)

INT. STUDENT BAR, UNIVERSITY OF BIRMINGHAM. NIGHT.
   The air's thick with smoke; excitable STUDENTS
crowd round a table bristling with empty beer
glasses shouting platitudes about writing. They're
all male, bar ONE BLONDE WOMAN in a leather jacket,
leaning back, arms folded.

What did I know about the theatre?

Compared with film, nothing. I'd grown up in a theatrical desert, with Rugby Theatre offering at best occasional amateur productions of Ira Levin 'thrillers'. Even my one chance to shine as actor playing Simon Chachava in Brecht's *The Caucasian Chalk Circle* (1944) at Sheriff was to be thwarted by a fire that burned down our venue as the show was about to open. We'd trundled with the school to see the odd RSC show in nearby Stratford but I found leather-clad men shouting incomprehensible verse into the deep pit of the stage pretty resistible.

Oxford had shifted that a little, mainly through my encounter with Pinter who powerfully bestrode the two worlds of film and theatre in his work with director Joseph Losey (*The Servant* (1963), *Accident* (1967)) as much as through my seeing his terse stage plays. Teaching had enabled me to consider myself a director as much as a writer, Brecht chief among my mentors. I went to Berlin in 1991 shortly after the Wall fell, seeking out his sober dwelling, the Brecht-Haus on the Chausseestrasse, where he lived with his wife Helene Weigel. Yet after the collapse of communism this winner of the Stalin Prize was in the doghouse and feminist scholarship by academics such as John Fuegi in *The Life and Lies of Bertolt Brecht* (1994) revealed my hero to be a predatory appropriator of his female assistants' work, from Elisabeth Hauptmann to Ruth Berlau.

What I had little or no experience of was of theatre *or* film as something written as well as filmed or staged. I'd swallowed whole the auteurist concept promulgated by the French *nouvelle vague* and critics like Andrew Sarris, that a film was authored by the director and screenwriting was a subordinate task. Even in this book I constantly attribute films to directors rather than writers, a habit I find hard to shake. Attending the MA in Playwriting in Birmingham helped to alter that.

As a West Midlander by origin it felt odd to be returning there. Birmingham had been the site of my forays to New Street railway station en route to gigs in the early

80s: Public Image Limited or U2 or Echo and the Bunnymen. Coventrians resent the shade thrown on them by their larger, younger neighbour, the town of a 'thousand trades' which exploded into Britain's second city in the Victorian era, graced with grandiose public architecture by Joseph Chamberlain, epitomised by the rusty megaliths of the University of Birmingham's Edgbaston campus, its tall Venetian tower named after him. The Department of Drama and Theatre Arts was located in the basement of a tower block, its venue, the Allardyce Nicoll Studio Theatre, named in honour of the department's founder. David Edgar was two years into the establishment of the first playwriting course in the UK there.

Edgar, who lived in nearby suburban Moseley, was a role model for what a writer might be. I'd first encountered him in *Marxism Today* where his urbane commentaries rubbed shoulders with the words of Stuart Hall, Eric Hobsbawm and Bea Campbell. But the figure on the sleeve of Methuen editions of his plays looked forbidding: wispy hair, beard, lit cigarette, cerebral frown. Edgar was the playwright-as-intellectual, literate in Gramsci and Lukacs, commanding the stages of our national institutions – but all I'd seen by him was the televised version of his epic adaptation of Dickens's *Nicholas Nickleby* from 1980.

I knew more about his peer David Hare, mainly because of Hare's ventures into film and television. Hare's 1985 film *Wetherby* made a deep impact on me, less from its torrid premise (a numb student, Tim McInnerny, blows out his brains in Vanessa Redgrave's kitchen) and more because it was a British realist film with political aspirations. Hare brought his reading of French film to bear on English emotional constipation and fashioned a haunting hybrid of stage and screen and his plays from *Knuckle* (1974) through to *Plenty* (1978) are likewise informed by manipulations of time and genre that are explicitly filmic. *Wetherby* improbably located Ian Holm, Judi Dench and Redgrave in a provincial town, but as director, Hare allowed them the space to improvise, loosening up their theatricality. And his Wetherby might well have been my Rugby; maybe Hare had finally met Truffaut's challenge.

We relocated to the stolid suburb of Hall Green, in a house run by Christian control freaks, adamant Hero and I shouldn't share a bed, which of course we did. We took dank walks up canals to the city's buffed-up town square, traced the edgelands that inspired Tolkien, ate cheap baltis in Balsall Heath and drove into the soft vales of Worcestershire. Then on Mondays and Tuesdays I learned about playwriting.

Edgar did not disappoint. He is a great teacher. It's hard to say exactly why, as his approach can tend to the formalist, this *soi-disant* Marxist sharing clips from Nora Ephron or Mel Brooks movies to tease out dramaturgical patterns. And we spent a long time making sense of the vocabulary he'd fashioned to describe them: what exactly was a 'format' in a scene? What might 'stretched time' look like in practice? He seemed happier to talk about Shakespeare or Rattigan than Brecht or Caryl Churchill. Yet week after week we witnessed him single-handedly inventing a discipline. Then there was his clubbability. David's tiny address book contained worlds; one week we'd walk into the seminar room to see Arnold Wesker awaiting us; the next, Sarah Daniels or Anne Devlin. His passion for playwriting was infectious, challenging the pre-eminence of the director, sitting through tedious Guild meetings ensuring writer's fees are up to snuff, enabling the rest of us rogues and romantics to thrive.

And he is a great playwright. I sat in the library working through decades of his work and the world revealed itself to me. The foundation of the NHS – David nailed that in *O Fair Jerusalem* (1975). The rise of British fascism? David was first off the block with *Destiny* (1976). The collapse of the Eastern bloc? Yup, an easy first again with *The Shape of the Table* (1990). His writing is a ceaseless set of engagements with a shifting reality subject to his keen craft and synthesising intellect.

Priggishly, I'd acquired the idea that writers were bookish intellectuals but my group, twelve strong, four woman and eight men, were more rock 'n' roll than that, happier in the bar than the library. Thankfully they knocked the shit out of me and none more so than an electrifying young playwright Sarah Kane. Then 22, fresh from super-trendy Drama at Bristol with peers such as Mark Ravenhill and David Greig, Saz, as we called her, up-ended all I knew about writing. Fierce, pierced, short shock of hair, red-lipped, Essex timbre inflecting her profanity, Sarah's love of confrontation made her hilarious, unpredictable company. Her feminism was instinctual and fearless, and we all fell foul of that fire.

This ferocity surfaced during a weekend workshop to which David invited one of his many pals, playwright Terry Johnson. This was thrilling largely because Terry's ingenious Stoppardian play *Insignificance* (1982) had been adapted to film by Nicolas Roeg in 1985. The play assembles anonymised versions of Einstein, Marilyn Monroe, Joe di Maggio and J. Edgar Hoover in a hotel room, and Roeg superimposed on it his preoccupation with synchronicity, flashing forward and back into the character's offstage lives with ruthless wit. Terry, pretty blithe about an experience I craved, revealed his first choice to direct was Louis Malle which struck me as amazingly cool. He was in his pomp and we were at his feet, as he showed us how to write active dialogue, applying the 'actioning' techniques of his mentor Max Stafford-Clark, who'd run the legendary Royal Court Theatre for the last decade.

We eagerly submitted work for him to explore with actors Nick Dunning and Julia LeGrand, to get the thrill of them drilling into our lines. This was my first exposure to the craft of working actors and I was avid to see them tear into my words and find them wanting. Sarah had submitted a monologue, a ferocious piece, elements of which resurfaced in her play *Crave* (1998). Johnson, leafing through at a '*table read*', frowned; he didn't seem to take to the play, as if there was something amiss with the writing. Sarah fought her corner as he set out to 'prove' that it didn't, couldn't work in that slightly brutal 'this-is-what-the-real-world-is-like' manner that a successful older man speaking to a young female writer in 1993 considered acceptable. Sarah, blushed, retrieved the script, Terry moved on. That was the end of that.

Later that night we were invited to join Johnson and the actors at David's home in Moseley. This was it! Fraternising with people in the industry! Everyone got drunk and the room fell quiet as Terry, also worse for wear, found himself at the wrong end of a harangue by an equally drunk Sarah about his masculinity, about his rubbish plays, his misguided direction, his dire workshop – staggered, and perhaps with admirable restraint, he let it wash over him.

We reconvened, hungover, the following morning for Day 2 of the workshop; Sarah submitted another piece. Terry, slightly green around the gills, distributed it to the actors. They began to read. The opening stage direction was not subtle: '*A woman stands over a man with a gun to his head.*' Johnson blanched; the actors cleared their throats and read on. Sarah sat, implacable. Terry confirmed that this, yes, was indeed a dramatic piece, no doubt about it. Point taken. You could feel the power dynamic in the room shift in real time from the man of the theatre to the young woman in her leather jacket and I'm convinced that day Sarah had embarked on her first and greatest play *Blasted* (1995) which in three years would propel us into the excitements of the '*in-yer-face*' movement that defined 1990s theatre just as surely as Britpop did its music. Yet what made Sarah different from other laddist challengers from Jez Butterworth to Patrick Marber was she was queer, and her work was informed by a fierce yet concrete morality, grounded in an unflinching image of her fellow humans.

Cinema was a presence that year even if theatre was our focus; and the venue combining both was the Midlands Arts Centre – the 'MAC' – in Cannon Hill Park, a vital lung in the shadow of the Edgbaston cricket ground. Back in the 60s Mike Leigh had made shows here; and nearby Pebble Mill BBC TV studios, where my childhood favourite *Rentaghost* was made, was home to *Second City Firsts*, half-hour dramas by writers such as Alan Bleasdale, Ian McEwan, directors like Les Blair, Mike Leigh, Stephen Frears, featuring actors such as Julie Walters and Alison Steadman, who performed TV's first lesbian kiss in one of them.

If Sarah taught me about contemporary theatre, I think I inducted her into cinema – together we saw Bergman's *Persona* (1965), surely the greatest film about theatre ever made; we saw Bunuel's *The Discreet Charm of the Bourgeoisie* (1972) and *The Exterminating Angel* (1962); but the film all of us spent the year defining ourselves against was *Reservoir Dogs* (1992). Partially this was because the presiding unacknowledged influence in the film was the playwright we also obsessed over, the belligerent, dazzling David Mamet, who straddled film and theatre. His plays made good films (*Glengarry Glen Ross* (1992)); his gripping cold films resembled strange airless plays (*House of Games* (1987), *Things Change* (1998), *Homicide* (1991)). On the horizon was his most divisive play, *Oleanna* (1992), making waves in America as a backlash against feminism on the liberal campus, with its hyper-real staccato dialogue and wilfully polarising male and female characters. My fellow male playwrights were besotted with him, their dialogue afflicted with Mamet-syndrome, coming out hyper-masculine, super-profane, talky, sweary and, as with Tarantino, riffing away in the shallows of pop culture.

And Tarantino showed that films were written before they were filmed; his irreverent macho banter defined the decade to come, unleashing unapologetic laddism into a culture where it'd been on the back foot. I've always found his aesthetic as a director appealing because of its theatrical emphasis. He relishes long-takes so the actors can hit their stride (and what actors – Keitel, Madsen, Buscemi, Roth); he draws courage from the stylisation of Godard as much as the example of pulp fiction or blaxploitation. The films reward reviewing, elicit re-enactment and offer decontextualised blokey role models: those dark shades, black ties, white shirts. Yes, Tarantino hit the etiolated cinema of the early 90s like a meteor.

Then there's the music: its incongruity, its geeky literacy, the facetious way it bounces off what we see while trapping us in the permanent cinematic past he fashions. Because Tarantino's films, for all their vernacular energy, care little for their moment and prefer to remain in an apolitical realm of the intertext. You learn almost nothing about 1992 from *Reservoir Dogs* as it denies any reality beyond the heist, the diner, the warehouse. This is determinedly retro, classical and abstract work, in that respect not unlike Mamet's later more hermetic plays.

And of course there's the film's violence. I'm sure the fierce debates around Tarantino's visceral taste for cruelty played some part in Sarah fashioning her own almost Jacobean theatre of violence; she once said, with a nod to Edward Bond, *'it's irresponsible not to write about violence'* and her work became synonymous with it. But the horrors in Sarah's plays – *Blasted* and *Cleansed* (1998) in particular - are an answer to a world of abuse and pain not a funky add-on. She was prescient about the atrocities about to be unloosed in former Yugoslavia or Rwanda – and the on-going sexual violence that Tarantino kept at bay, as if it might sully his balletic interest in it.

I found his flip, aestheticized approach to representation – at once shockingly real and yet held at a jokey distance – a barrier to admiration. Having grown up around violence in a way that I hadn't even noticed and having consumed it uncritically in film, I set myself an interdiction against it in my writing. For me the eye-catching, ear-severing, Stealers Wheel-playing relish for it in *Reservoir Dogs* has made me a doubtful Tarantino-watcher ever since. I loved *Jackie Brown* (1997), and long stretches of *Once Upon a Time in Hollywood* (2019), but the callowness of anything from *Inglorious Basterds* (2009) to *Kill Bill* whichever part, the deployment of his great talent to tell all-too-trite macho tales, increasingly leaves me cold. At bottom Tarantino provoked a profound debate about the role of violence in all art: is it emetic in function or is it there to provide pleasure? Madsen's louche prowl round his prey has prompted emulation in a thousand films that seek to make torture a screen tease in a celebration not a critique of male power. Is it fair to note the centrality of newcomer producer Harvey Weinstein to the film's closed circuit of masculine energy?

The year ended with a two-week rehearsal and presentation of our plays performed by students. I'd embarked on an opaque project called *The Pact*, an allegory about the European Union which my tutor, the playwright Clare McIntyre – who, given her play *Low Level Panic* (1988) is a classic of feminist theatre, I foolishly undervalued – didn't know what to do with. Edgar was brought in to confirm I was creating something that simply didn't communicate; I plaintively declared, *'I just don't want to be obvious'*; his response was lethal: *'I don't think that's going to be your problem.'*

So *The Pact* was set aside and with it my illusions about theatre as a place to parade your own cleverness. Yet I'd been very taken with the reflections of guest playwright Trevor Griffiths talking about his 1978 translation of Chekhov's *The Cherry Orchard*. Griffiths spanned theatre, television and film, managing to maintain his serious voice in all media. For all of his avowed socialist commitments, which inform his play *The Party* (1973), he'd written the screenplay for Warren Beatty's blockbuster *Reds* (1981), and for director Richard Eyre written *Country* (1981) a '*TV masterpiece*' in the words of John Weaver. A startling transposition of Chekhov to an English country house on the eve of the Labour victory in 1945, it subtly alludes to the ascent of Thatcher, intent on reversing what ensued. The writing is cool in its sympathies, without directly condemning the dominion of the country set; if this had been a film with a theatrical release it would have been acclaimed as a defining work of the era – as ever British television simply tossed it out and moved on. Nevertheless, Griffiths's example drove me back to an engagement with the naturalism I had discounted. Likewise the subtle supportive work for the small screen of underrated TV writer Paula Milne focused me on detail I had overlooked; her patient and generous assistance with my work went beyond the call of duty and the confines of the course.

Not that the resulting play *Utopians* was in anything like the same league; it was still caught between film and stage, layering two stories into one household and seeking to dramatise 'everyday life' in the manner of Godard but playing more like a weirder Alan Ayckbourn. This time I was to be the beneficiary of Terry Johnson's skilled and subtle direction, as he tried to untangle the knots I'd created in the play which as he noted I had '*dreamed up*'.

But we were all upstaged that weekend by the first act of *Blasted* which, setting aside the violence, blew apart the consensus that a play must articulate its meaning, observe leftist decorums of representation in language and maintain naturalistic integrity. Sarah showed us all the way, and even if it was not my way, I knew it would define the future we all faced.

The debut of its first act in a hot Allardyce Nicoll Studio Theatre was charged with rumour; her portrait of a profane middle-aged tabloid journalist and a young epileptic woman in a Leeds hotel left the audience in awed silence. Could you actually show that? A blow-job that ends in Cate biting Ian's dick? An act of violation after she fits? And all this playing out in unforgiving real time? In London three years later it would prompt walk-outs and reviews proclaiming it a '*feast of filth*'.

After Birmingham Sarah and I saw each other less and less; we'd meet at the Bush Theatre where she was a script reader; I saw her flanked by men at the bar in the Royal Court the night I went to see *Blasted*. I last saw her performing Grace in *Cleansed* as she stood in for Suzan Sylvester who'd done her back in in the show. Sarah was no actor – she always played herself. Here she was pale and monotone, intoning her words with little inflection, lost in the great stage of the Duke of York to a thinly attended house. The following year I was in a residency in Lumb Bank, Yorkshire, on a snowy February day, when the news came through that she'd taken her own life after a period of sustained depression; suddenly her flaring up of anger, her sheer intensity, her tendency to go missing, made retrospective sense. In her all too short life, she changed what a play might be and what a writer might do forever.

10 *Winter Light*: Marriage Story

(CAMBRIDGE)

EXT. ST. MARY'S CHURCH, GREAT SHELFORD. AFTERNOON.
In the pews a hundred or so people sit hushed,
awaiting the arrival of the bride; among them A MAN
in a linen suit, eyes riveted on the altar. Bach
plays from the organ loft.

I've never thought of my life as especially peripatetic but the last eight chapters give the lie to that. But in the mid 90s I committed to a person and place that define me to this day.

Commitment, like happiness, in the words of de Montherlant, *'writes in white ink on a white page'*. And why get married in an age of seriality, metrosexuality, deferred commitments? The symptomatic stories of the mid 1990s are flat-share group comedies – *Friends, Seinfeld, Sex and the City*. The apartment with obligatory sofa hosts the pseudo-family from which our hero ventures out into a bottomless well of choices; plenty more fish in the sea! (Which, with barely a fish to be found these days, now rings pretty hollow.) Yet I headed in the opposite direction. Why?

For some marriage is irredeemably tainted by patriarchy or in Engels' analysis, the ballast of capitalism; certainly it coexists uneasily with film just as film and settlement are antithetical. In a movie there's always another horizon, a door swinging ajar onto another reality. As John Wayne walks through the homesteaders' portal at the close of John Ford's *The Searchers* (1956), his restlessness expresses the predicament of the cinematic hero – journeying into the world not into the self. The road movie, the adventure movie and the western are driven by a craving for movement out from what Christopher Vogler dubs *'the ordinary world'* on into the endless journey. Yet maybe there are other kinds of journey; maybe there are other kinds of film.

The course ended; I was broke and in debt. I went for a job at Hills Road Sixth Form College on the fringe of Cambridge. It was a long shot; I'd thrown over my promising career for an MA and a Career Development Loan during John Major's slump. Yet amazingly, I got it.

I had no form with Cambridge. I'd never even visited it. From afar the university seemed forbidding, its English faculty for whom Hero would teach once home to Raymond Williams, Colin MacCabe, George Steiner, martyrs to the astringent legacy of F. R. Leavis. But Cambridge is more than the university. The colleges, like pearls on a necklace, coil round the Cam, glimpsed through porter's lodges excluding the city's citizens, except to clean or cater to them. Cambridge is bipolar, its shopping districts are neatly divided, the inner core of high-end chains, the less affluent unsubtly directed from the bus station to chain stores in the 'kite' district. The two worlds are designed never to meet.

The other Cambridge drew me, onto the open land threading out to Stourbridge Common where streets such as Garlic Row memorialise the site of one of Europe's largest medieval fairs (prototype for Bunyan's 'Vanity Fair'). Or the pert loaf of the Leper Chapel facing a football ground, marking the city limits where the indigent were kept at bay.

Hills Road was governed by its head Colin Greenhalgh as a minor city state. With many teachers graced with PhDs it had pretensions beyond its further education status. Greenhalgh, who imagined it an Oxbridge college, chafed at the fact I refused to wear a tie and allowed students to call me 'Steve'. Ties loomed large for him; he began each academic year by announcing to the new cohort that he possessed 365 ties and if any of them were to catch him wearing the same tie two days in a row a reward of £50 awaited them. The reward, to my knowledge, was never awarded.

Yes, I was a teacher again but now I had a kind of power as I stepped into the shoes of my predecessor Roger Dalladay, who'd run the Department of Performing Arts for thirty years. Roger was a satyr-bearded polymath responsible for a continuous repertoire of theatre-making who directed, adapted, acted, choreographed, even designed his sets, painting flats in his underpants before the show went up. His Hellenistic taste frequently took him into the realms of Dionysus; hence the cardboard box in the costume cupboard labelled '*Roger's Todgers*', containing a sad heap of polyester phalluses.

Yes, here was responsibility and good work; and, as I turned 30, I was ready for it, seeking purpose, pattern, even ritual. I had a theatre to run, my own personal '*train-set*' as Orson Welles once said of his films. Brick walled, black dance floor, raked auditorium, flat stage like an anatomy theatre, high white rear wall curved into a cyclorama. This was my kingdom, smelling of dust burnt in the heat of the lights.

In the next three years I directed Aphra Behn (*The Rover* (1677)), Shakespeare (*The Tempest* (1610), *As You Like It* (1599)), J. M. Synge (*Riders to the Sea* (1904)), Brian Friel (*Translations* (1980)), Jim Cartwright (*Road* (1986)), Friedrich Durrenmatt (*The Visit* (1956)), Bryony Lavery (*More Light* (1997)), Brecht (*Happy End* (1929)), Timberlake Wertenbaker (*Our Country's Good* (1988)), not to mention *Fiddler on the Roof* (1964) and the plays of a certain S. Waters. My team was maverick stage manager Darren, dynamic dance teacher Hazel, and Jane, a costume-maker who lurked in a Nissen hut full of taffeta – and legions of students. Each year they poured in from local schools, bursting with talent, hungry for experience, wired with expectation. Like the manic backlot of a Hollywood studio set we'd cast, rehearse and stage play after play until we were dizzy – raise the steel-deck! Hang that gauze! What's the play again? It cured me of any desire to be Peter Hall or Peter Brook. Theatre management was less about theory and more about scaff towers, gaffer tape and balanced budgets. Directing was less about *v-effekts* and '*biomechanics*' and more a matter of stand there, stick this on, say this, go! Yet making theatre exempted me from other questions; each day the task was clear and the year's rhythms were marked out in one show after another, one lesson after another.

Suddenly, with work in place and income regular, settling down was in sight; but was this a cop-out? I was a solvent urban professional living with Hero. Nothing alerts you to domestic life until it's shared. Furniture, meals, bedtimes, sex, nights out, bank balances, families – all become gripping fulcrums. My parents were relieved I'd got a partner but they hadn't bargained for a feminist legitimately taking umbrage at dad's anxious jokes – such as the occasion when Hero declined a proffered whisky eliciting his aside: '*Cheap to run, Steve.*'

We moved to a scruffy house on Mill Road, which, as a Cambridge don explained to me, was '*a splinter of Hackney*' aimed at the city. Certainly there were South Asian, Chinese and Italian eateries, all the amenities of multicultural living amid the railway workers' terraced houses gentrified by academics and artists. If we bought a house together surely the next step was obvious. Nevertheless I resisted marriage, coldly citing how '*I can only love in the moment given my lack of faith in futurity*'. This caveat turned to ash in my mouth when on a ferry heading out of Plymouth Hoe for Spain, I found myself blurting four words nobody owns: '*Will you marry me?*' Hero, inured to my pleas of how my lack of faith in futurity meant I could only assert love in the moment, was speechless. Thankfully she smiled and the sea dazzled in sympathy.

Coincidentally, this declaration was followed by a screening of *Four Weddings and a Funeral* (1994) in the boat's bowels. Given the ship's lurch as we crossed the Bay of Biscay this proved to be a nauseating experience, and not merely thanks to Hugh Grant's ingratiating mannerisms. Mike Newell and Richard Curtis nailed the zeitgeist in their conjuration of a boho metropolitan set, the solo working-class gay alibi of John Hanna there to offset any smugness. But alongside the flat-share comedy, romcom dominated the screens, ranging from the profound (Ang Lee and Emma Thompson's *Sense and Sensibility* (1995), Rob Reiner and Nora Ephron's *When Harry Met Sally* (1989)) to the anodyne or the repellent (*Pretty Woman*, (1990), *Notting Hill* (1999)). I resisted these fables of heterosexual desire working their variations on the 'marriage plot' for a world in which monogamy and marriage were both in question and love seemed more governed by genes and accident than providence.

But I had made my choice and it didn't feel wrong. Those childless years of two incomes in the becalmed mid 90s look impossibly privileged now. We stepped onto the property ladder with some strain but nothing compared to our young equivalents now. This was the crest of the first wave of globalisation when the economy was deemed by cheerleaders such as Geoff Mulgan to function on '*thin air*'. To marry was to invest in the hope of that moment, to follow the example of our parents, fusing our very lives.

And Cambridge was Hero's home. In committing to her I gained a new family, throwing in my lot with her five siblings as if wandering into a Chekhov play mid-show. I was a latecomer to the story; Hero's father Theo, a brilliant medic, had died far too young of cancer a decade earlier. The Chalmers family was now defined by Hero's mother Doreen, or 'Orn' as she was known, living alone in a half-timbered house whose lawns descended to the shallows of the Cam. This world seemed a world away from my world, yet it felt like coming home.

Orn, at first sight archetypally English educated middle class, was in fact a former nurse and defiant non-conformist, her cerebral Anglicanism self-taught. Her faith was about deeds and observance, and her stewardship of St Mary's, the parish church of Great Shelford, defined that. Every dawn she threw open the church's heavy medieval doors to enter its spectral stone light (in fact so regular was she in this task that a decade later she featured en route in no less than two Google Streetview images). She knew every inch of its interior from the spidery washed-out horrors of the Doom painting shimmering out of the plaster (like the image of hell and heaven revealed by Colin Firth in Pat O'Connor's fine film of J. L. Carr's novella *A Month in the Country* (1987)) to the brasses of village luminaries or the spiky coral of the rood screen. Her fastidious sense of ritual, her askesis, by which she held the various vicars who passed through to account, fused the aesthetic and the ethical and I found it inspiring. But it also mirrored the concerns of a film that came to matter deeply to me, Ingmar Bergman's *Winter Light* (1963), also known as *The Communicants*. Here in filmic language, I recognised her passion and maybe my own.

Bergman's startling real-time opening unfolds an act of communion. I've always been an antsy observer of ceremony, bored at the liturgy, wanting to call out its solemnity, in prayer only hearing the roar of myself. Here in Bergman's cold-eyed images of the pastor's tiny embattled congregation seen from the altar steps, we see four communicants joylessly engaged in rote-acts, who echoed the ageing and infirm congregation of Shelford at prayer. Yes, this was parochial life as commitment, but also an image of human infirmity, Nietzsche's vision of Christianity as a '*slave-religion*' fuelled by *ressentiment*.

The pastor (Gunnar Bjornstrand) gazes over his worshippers with little piety and undisguised boredom. In showing his predicament Bergman knew of what he spoke - his own father, Erik, was a retired pastor whose vocation went so deep that, on arriving one Sunday at a church in Uppsala where the resident cleric declared himself too ill to officiate, he took it upon himself to take the ceremony. Bjornstrand's wintry servicing of a dying faith is grimly recorded as his day unfolds, going on to receive an abject supplicant (Max Von Sydow) who is paralysed by existentialist anxiety. The pastor's failure to offer the man comfort seems to provokes his subsequent suicide – and given this is Bergman, the film starts bleak and descends into beyond bleak. Its central scene is entirely wordless; the camera views the pastor in long-shot, helpless at the scene of suicide, his ministrations obliterated by the river's indifferent sussurations.

Yet while the film refuses any easy redemption, it still reaches a place beyond mere doubt by honouring the idea of a vocation without reward. Yes, God may be silent, and yes, the pastor's work gains neither affirmation nor acclaim; but his predicament is used by Bergman to celebrate the vocation of art-making as an end in itself regardless of applause or approval. As he wrote in *The Making of Film, 'I do my work for everyday purposes not for eternity and my pride is the pride of a good craftsman.*' The pastor honours his craft by being there at the death whatever his inner doubts, and for Bergman that's enough. Years later the film's steely vision informed my play *Temple* (2015) which examined the agony of the Dean of St Paul's Cathedral after he closes the church during the Occupy encampment at its doors in 2011.

Bergman's passion for wedlock is unarguable – after all he got married five times. His career is grounded in the pains and joys of commitment, however rooted in uneven power. This is also evident in his loyalty to his company of actors (von Sydow, Bjornstrand, Ingrid Thulin, Liv Ullmann, Bibi Andersson, Erlin Josephsson), his cinematographer Sven Nykvist, his alternation between cinema and theatre and his attachment to Sweden. Like with his great predecessor Ibsen's plays, each film asks a question that provokes the next, even if the aesthetic language retains a common severity. *Winter Light* is generally lumped in with its predecessors *Through a Glass Darkly* (1961) and *The Silence* (1963), as a calmer consideration of morality untethered from an absent deity. Does any other film-maker uses film to think through their commitments so systematically? I binged on his work to unlock my own life.

These were hardly bankable concerns in the headlong blissed-out 90s when every play or film gleefully showcased druggy transgression, even if, as in Mark Ravenhill's symptomatic *Shopping and Fucking* (1996), it is offset by an underlying sadness. Ravenhill's gang of white kids named for the member of Take That and living off junk food and ecstasy in a featureless London embodied the drift into blank hedonism. In cinema this was epitomised by the films of Danny Boyle whose movies promised sexy British cinema as never before. Yet from this vantage films such as *Shallow Grave* (1994) and *Trainspotting* (1996) for all their panache seem symptomatic of the hyperbole of 'Cool Britannia'. Again they're '*in-yer-face*' in-crowd affairs, all flat-sharing and needle-sharing, transmuted through Boyle's showy aesthetic into lifestyle primers with gorgeous young male British actors modelling junkie chic, free of family, class or place. Just as Oasis's self-pitying whine fell short of their heroes The Beatles, Boyle's whizzy sub-Tarantino movies too often resemble sixties predecessors *Georgy Girl* (1966) or *Alfie* (1966) in their bid for zeitgeist cooldom.

That spirit was cultivated by so-called New Labour ready to storm the nation in May 1997 – and I count that night as one of the greatest in my life. But Tony Blair's shiny embrace of modernising even then rang false. Where was the ecological consciousness provoked by the challenge of climate change, which surfaced at United Nations intergovernmental summits at Rio de Janeiro (1992) and later Kyoto (1997)? It found little traction in a decade obsessed with growth and open borders. I found myself inspired by the injunction to '*Think Global, Act Local*'; after years of being nowhere for long, aloof from anything that resembled place, I resolved to take strength from locality.

But what did the local offer? In East Anglia, and South Cambridgeshire in particular, agri-business subordinated the fenland landscape into dark earthed monoculture. Walking this new domain, paths trickled out into nothingness and private and corporate ownership prevailed in a landscape of denuded peat and tiny pockets of embattled nature, politically conservative, with Cambridge a liberal island within it. Was this to be my place?

Film helped orientate me; cinema embodies the pivot between the local and the global and since 1977 Cambridge had become a recognised destination on cinema's atlas thanks to its annual film festival at the Arts Cinema. The Arts was a dark enclave at the rear of Market Passage, opened in 1947 as a 'temple' of cinema and closed in 1999. You'd queue up in rain or snow before being admitted into its dark tunnel, a distinct whiff of the sewers seeping up from under the seats. Yet here the global met the local and here was to be my temple and my ritual.

The festival epitomised summer, taking place in July as the school term was winding down; we'd dive into the dark and return like Orpheus to the light to swim in Jesus Green Lido or eat ice cream. But what was the credo there? For film so often seemed to stand in the place vacated by faith. How else to explain the pleasure and necessity of spending two long afternoons lost in the maze of Jacques Rivette's six-hour epic *Jeanne la Pucelle* (1994) which established Sandrine Bonnaire as in the same league as Jeanne Falconetti in the role of Joan in Carl Dreyer's masterpiece *La Passion de Jeanne d'Arc* (1928) or the excitement of another defining account of martyrdom, Robert Bresson's *Procès de Jeanne d'Arc* (1962) – film's gaze was as rapt and redemptive as any religious gesture. And the films of Bresson in particular, who died in 1999, summed up this fusion of ritual, of the real and the local, defining film's realm.

Bresson stringently avoided of '*filmed theatre*'; for him the '*terrible habit of the theatre*' was to be avoided by the guiding presence of film's primary artist, which he called the '*cinematographer*' not the director. As with his students such as Douglas or Godard this insight is derived from the nature of the actor, differentiating him from Bergman's ensemble approach. Bresson's preference, rather like Beckett's, was for actors who disavow '*interpretation*', and this preference lead him to favour non-professional '*models*' for their lack of studiedness, their creaturely qualities, to become avatars of their settings. Bresson was seeking to create an art beyond conscious will: '*Films can only be made by by-passing the will of those who appear in them, using not what they do, but what they are.*' Like Bergman's pastor who acts without hope or intent, Bresson's actors simply exist rather than signify. We barely recall the names of the figures who populate his films, gauche and heavy with self-consciousness, compelled by him to repeat their gestures until purged of artifice; whereas Bergman looked his players in the eye, Bresson's actors are as figural as icons.

In theatre characters so often articulate themselves in language leaving no equivalent for a film such as Bresson's *Au Hasard Balthazar* (1966) which tracks the mute suffering of a donkey as it travels from hand to hand, with the equivalence he grants to humans and landscapes. His minimalist aesthetic, with sound heightened and diegetic music largely banished, except as a kind of choric commentary – say, the resurgent opening chords of Mozart's Mass in C Minor that punctuate the austere rituals of imprisonment and escape in *Un Condamné à Mort est Échappé*

(1956) – may seem to threaten airless control, but these devices meld into something approaching the transcendent. Here we see humans as natural forms; nature as humanly conceived.

Bresson's compassionate gaze links him with his peers Tarkovsky and Bergman, and his influence is still felt in films like Chloe Zhao's *The Rider* (2017) which directs its steady gaze at a young man and his horse illuminating a life language barely reaches. The mesmerising power of physical action in Bresson's work – the spoon steadily scraping the prison wall in *A Man Escaped*, the suicidal girl Mouchette rolling repeatedly down a slope, the clash of armour in the joust in *Lancelot du Lac* (1974) – amounts to a kind of liturgy which disavows God but is committed to redemption. Bresson's self-denying ordinances resist film's potential to dominate just as the self-denials of the Dogme movement initiated by Lars von Trier in 1995 were intended to do. While in that case those renunciations felt gestural, in Bresson's work they underwrite a desire to create contemplation.

The day we got married it was hot and dry; even the air seemed festive. The ceremony was in St Mary's, the reception in a marquee in Orn's garden. Hero's sister Sophie arranged for flowers to erupt from its poles; mum made the layered cake. It was a handmade occasion (as Tilda Swinton said of her friend Derek Jarman's work, there was *'a whiff of the school play'*). The ringers set the bells pealing and when I walked into the cool of the church and saw the entire dramatis personae of my life there I was nearly paralysed by it, as if trespassing on my own funeral. What followed was nothing to do with God even if it took place in a house dedicated to him, but it was everything to do with love and commitment. Mum took it upon herself to film it all on the VCR; dad threatened to make a 'comic' speech, donning joke glasses and getting a big laugh. My sister and her new husband brought her two young kids, my nephew and niece. Hero's siblings – Sophie, Clarissa, Roger and Frances – sat among years of shared friends and family. My family and Hero's family, my life and her life, together in the taut air, redolent of tarpaulin.

From here, mid-90s Cambridge feels like a lost world of optimism, but in the midst of its apparent stability suddenly I was writing. After Bresson I reached back for other models of dramas rooted in place, Rossellini's films, his miscellany set in the misty Po valley, *Paisan* (1946), his documenting of devastated Berlin, *Germany: Year Zero* (1948). Or Michelangelo Antonioni's films, their ethereal gaze shifting from human dramas into the life of things, especially *L'Avventura* (1960), in which a woman goes missing on a volcanic island without that mystery ever being resolved.

I wrote a monologue I called 'Drive' about a woman driving away from her new child, her husband and her work into eastern England by something beyond her comprehension; I followed her husband in pursuit – in the midst of happiness I wrote about the disintegration of happiness. I called the play *English Journeys* (1998), dubbed it a road movie for the stage. I sent it to the Bush Theatre, the Royal Court and the Hampstead, the three main new writing theatres. I resolved that if none of them responded positively I was not a writer and should set those hopes aside.

Act Three Writing

11 *Code Unknown*: Cosmopolis

(LONDON)

INT. HAMPSTEAD THEATRE, SWISS COTTAGE LONDON. MORNING.
The bar's quiet; the artistic team huddle round a table laden with a pile of scripts.

1999. Through the windows of the Portakabin structure I can see a scruffy market and traffic interchange as Finchley Road descends into the maelstrom of central London. Ghosts are everywhere – up there on Avenue Road, Beckett's chief director Alan Schneider was killed by a motorbike while crossing the road. In the auditorium to my left, reached by a small riser of stairs, audiences watched John Malkovich in Lanford Wilson's *Burn This* (1987), alongside debuts by Pinter, Sam Shepard, Mike Leigh and Shelagh Stephenson.

I am the theatre's playwright-in-residence; every week I sit with the artistic team filleting a heap of plays, the same slush pile from which I was retrieved a year earlier. We drink coffee and give our reports, the meeting chaired by deeply brainy literary manager Ben Jancovich. We generally find ourselves awaiting the arrival of artistic director Jenny Topper who sweeps in with flowers and cakes, startling in her elan, and legendary for her stewardship of new writing theatres, a familiar of Alan Rickman and Lindsay Duncan and everyone else you could think of.

Also there is director Gemma Bodinetz, who expertly ushered in my first play *English Journeys* last year, a stage road movie eliciting tart reviews such as, '*Pull over and let this one pass*'. Opposite is Scottish playwright Rona Munro who's recently collaborated with Ken Loach on *Ladybird, Ladybird* (1994). This is a *very* exciting meeting. We gossip and feel that flush of power that comes with presiding over the fate of other people's plays – plays arriving via agents, or success on other continents. I can still feel the excitement of reading a draft of Australian writer Andrew Bovell's *Speaking in Tongues* (1996), a fractured tale from the edge of a city he went on to adapt into *Lantana* (2001). Writing, acting and directing careers begin in the meetings such as this and this is the beginning of mine.

It's my turn to report on a text by a well-thought-of writer and someone, unbeknownst to me, beloved to Jenny. The play's a commission, so a lot rides on it; this is a second draft – we are in a culture of '*intervention*' where plays can languish for years. My next play *After the Gods* (2002) even as we speak is going through draft after draft, gradually becoming more diffuse in effect. And the play before us is a muddled, self-indulgent affair, as if written in code rather than aimed at the audience. I clear my throat and read out my response, concluding, with high diplomacy:

'There's clearly a place for all this inventive wildness and vigour but I found the framework so indecipherable that the play became dull and arbitrary.'

As I look up, I realise I've committed a terrible faux pas. Have I struck the right note? Ben refuses my gaze; Gemma has to take a call; Rona's rummaging in her bag. As Jenny's summoned away to her next meeting, she announces, *'Well, we're doing it, darling.'*

As ever I have missed out on a key plot detail; I've never been great at plot.

But I'm here to learn and I am in London, a city I've wilfully, even ignorantly avoided. Partially this is the result of life choices, partially a residual provincialism which makes me resent the notion that anything of worth must pass through London and little of worth exists out of it. Partially it's because I am only now in my 30s recognising London as a place where artists concentrate, a network and a hub. As a latecomer I'm constantly trespassing on places where the professional and the personal mysteriously combine.

Hampstead Theatre still looks like a fringe endeavour, but a new building is in train. It's a less trendy address than the newly reopened Royal Court in Sloane Square or the media-friendly Soho Theatre, or even the the Bush in West London. Jenny's forever having charm offensive lunches with critics. Hampstead plays like Hampstead novels get confounded with perceptions of an audience which is deemed bourgeois, perhaps with a tint of racism, given its loyal and largely Jewish audience.

But I delight in its non-corporate, personal ethos, this flimsy two-storey structure set down amid fly-blown park, community centre and swimming pool, summer's scent emerging from underground vents. I bus there from my pied-à-terre with friends Sophie and Andrew in Highgate imagining myself part of this cosmopolis. The theatre team back then now seems unforgivably white, yet during my time Hampstead launches writers such as Roy Williams and Tanika Gupta and its education programme takes me into diverse schools from Uxbridge to Tower Hamlets. Yes, it is unashamedly middle class in clientele and work but equally it's delighted to take risks, and I am one of those risks.

My residency unfolds as the new millennium arrives. New Labour are in their pomp; Tony Blair's beginning his taste for *'liberal interventionism'*, small wars with *'progressive'* political aims, now going sour as NATO clumsily weighs in in Kosovo. London's the shop window of his 'Third Way' as off-the-books accounting results in new hospitals and, under my old JCR president David Miliband, academy schools; and the Jubilee Line is being extended to accommodate the cultural vacuum that is the Millennium Dome. Its grey strip is my road map, whisking me from Swiss Cottage into the heart of the city.

There I'm part of a writing group called Paines Plough led by Vicky Featherstone and Mark Ravenhill, deputised to write a play for each new station. We meet in their cold office four floors up over Aldwych. Mark, enormously tall, shaved head, presides like a kindly elder brother. debbie tucker green, hooped earrings, arresting smile, is one of us, a stage manager at the Royal Court, and after Winsome Pinnock, an all-too-rare female playwright of African-Caribbean heritage who'll go on to be the most important dramatist of the decade with plays like *born bad* (2003), *generation* (2005) and *random* (2010), and direct and write *Second Coming* (2014), a mystical account of a BAME family which allows its stars Nadine Marshall and Idris Elba a space of rare ambiguity and openness. Anyway, we're all allocated Tube stops on the new line to inspire us. Scathing satirist Simon Smith, successor to me as resident writer at Hampstead, writes a lethally funny piece about working-class racism in West Ham. My designated Tube stop's London Bridge. South of the river is entirely new to me, with its weave of ethnicities and classes, brutalist estates, wholesale markets, the remnants of the Liberties. I traverse it trying to take its measure, break its code.

Part of this is a long-overdue reckoning with multiculturalism. I grew up between diverse Midland cities and white-only villages, with British South Asian and East Asian friends, whose survival strategy was a relentless jokiness at their own expense. Oxford hardly helped correct that bias nor teaching in schools largely in what one educationalist called '*the white highlands*'. The reality of London and the encounter with writers – and eventually directors - of colour provoked me into using writing as a way out of that parochialism of the mind.

Writing permitted me a free pass into the city: lunching at the canteen of the National on the South Bank, a meet-and-greet at a TV company in Shoreditch, rehearsing in Kilburn. My first gestures at writing the pluralism of the city were wild approximations. In my London-based plays such as *Little Platoons* (2011), *Temple* or *Limehouse* I tried to scale down the city to a focal point I could understand: a cathedral resting on a millennium of urban life, a free school reflecting the fractures of its own post code, the gentrified kitchen of David and Debbie Owen with its back to the river. Decoding London as layer upon layer of worlds, palimpsests, ecosystems was my way to crack it open, A-Z in hand.

Ken Livingstone, now reviled because of inane anti-Semitic remarks, back then was offering a reboot of the municipal socialism he first promulgated in the 1980s. The dotcom bubble had yet to burst and London's artists were yet to be priced out by the insanity of capital flows. Its new centre seemed to be Canary Wharf as much as Trafalgar Square. And one of the recipients of New Labour largesse was culture – theatre and film.

I see London through the lens of film; even the cinema venue I most often patronise, the Renoir in the Brunswick complex in Bloomsbury, features in a movie, Antonioni's *The Passenger* (1975); his earlier film *Blow-Up* (1966) – from Edward Bond's screenplay - moving from Notting Hill into Bond's manor of South London, defines the mysterious underside of the city. I wander past my agent Micheline Steinberg's fourth-floor offices on Great Portland Street (I have an agent! She even has the sort of office you might expect an agent to have, full of scripts, posters and DVDs) dipping into BBC Broadcasting House, or amble along the Thames Path sensing ghostly landscapes of early Hitchcock or Ealing films. The late-90s screen was awash with lottery-funded zeitgeisty romcoms or crime heists (*The Low Down* (2001), *Rancid Aluminium* (2000)), or works of geezer gangsterism from Guy Ritchie or Richard

Curtis's mythologizing of West London, unimprovably first captured in Roeg and Cammell's dazzling rebus of a film, *Performance* (1970).

Away from red buses and Big Ben, coke deals and bank heists, the 90s had seen more nuanced attempts to capture the drift and pain of urban life. Michael Winterbottom's haunting *Wonderland* (1998) explores love and family south of the river as does Gary Oldman's ferocious account of his Greenwich childhood, *Nil by Mouth* (1997), releasing Ray Winstone and Kathy Burke from the perennial sentimental filter through which working-class London life gets viewed. Yet even these fine films fall short of addressing the complex multiculturalism of the city; perhaps London defies exhaustive representation. Only Iain Sinclair's psychogeographic audits in *Lights Out for the Territory* (1997) get near the haunted nature of the city, street by street, house by house, or Patrick Keiller's quirky Paul Schofield-narrated *London* (1994), a fictive essay and riddle, its poised gaze tracking the rise of Docklands and the interaction of capital and Capital.

The model for any urban film or play of the last days of the last millennium was Robert Altman's *Short Cuts* (1993) in its account of the complexity of a large metropolitan area, in his case Los Angeles. Altman's portmanteau approach solders together the short stories of Raymond Carver, displacing them from the Pacific Northwest into a spliced account of sexuality, neighbourhood and grief loosely unified through an earthquake. I'd seen it in Paris, devastated by its heedless juxtapositions of tragedy and comedy, its dazzling ensemble cast defining the go-to actors of the next generation – Sean Penn, Julianne Moore, Matthew Broderick, Jennifer Jason Leigh. But amazingly its focus was still exclusively white experience, something the later, far less potent *Crash* (2004) at least seeks to redress.

Altman's epic social vision reveals the city as a place of collision and evasion, pioneered in his two masterpieces, *The Long Goodbye* (1973) and *Nashville* (1975), the latter nicely described by Wim Wenders as '*a movie about noise*'. By splintering soundtrack and image and viewing its cast in deep focus, these seminal films sidle round LA in the wake of Elliot Gould's louche private investigator or turn the capital of Country into an audit of America in its bicentennial year. Here, and again in *Short Cuts*, Altman fashions a serene, liberal yet misanthropic sense of the city as an '*infinitely suffering thing*' as T. S. Eliot put it. His influence was apparent theatrically in Patrick Marber's and David Hare's reboots of Schnitzler's *La Ronde* (1897), *Closer* (1997) and *The Blue Room* (1998), which fashion urban labyrinths of sexuality and money but are limited by their self-conscious bids for 'urbanity'.

Short Cuts spawned a wave of imitations, most notably Paul Thomas Anderson's brilliant but callow *Magnolia* (1999), but for me the most significant was a European rejoinder, Michael Haneke's elliptical, chilly *Code Unknown* (2000). Haneke's film offered a darker lens with which to view the Western city of migration, injustice, hinting at the underside of New Labour's moderating project. As the last great European auteur Haneke had moved from theatre to a run of devastatingly austere films giving the lie to the optimism of the 90s. His first major urban work, *71 Fragments of a Chronology of Chance* (1994),and its title alone announced his scepticism at film's legibility. Urban reality is not *'explicable'* as is evident in his splintered vision of Vienna, organised around the defining image of 1990s *anomie*, a random shooting, apparently the only unifying tissue for a society that refuses solidarity. Haneke's best films, *The White Ribbon* (2009) and *Amour* (2012), are yet to come. Unifying them all, from the rather monolithic and aggressive early critiques of film violence such as *Benny's Video* (1992) and the unwatchable *Funny Games* (1997), is a cinema of high seriousness and implacable clarity, its action pitched beyond the characters' viewpoints, subjecting them to ordeals of judgement which the audience too can only submit to.

Code Unknown is set in Paris, where Haneke had relocated, just as the European Union acceded to new post-communist nations and was venturing into the Eurozone. It anatomises the profoundly unequal society that was coming into being, juxtaposing media types such as Juliette Binoche's footloose actress (a role she repeats in his next film *Cache*) with the beleaguered toing and froing of Romanian migrants into the city and the struggles against racism of Amadou, a young man of sub-Saharan heritage. Haneke breaks his episodes into fragments via black-outs, refusing the *'totality'* Altman forges in his films, offering wilfully, *'incomplete tales of several journeys'* as his subtitle suggests. The central conceit is of parallel experiences that move indifferently, even hostilely past each other. These fractures are epitomised in the horribly real scene in which Binoche is verbally abused on the Metro by a young man of North African descent, her set features and the disengagement of her fellow passengers captured in the steely glare of Jurgen Jurges's disinterested camera. A crackle of aggression informs every shot, questioning naive narratives of diversity underpinning the heyday of Blairism. In a year 9/11 would change that forever and Haneke's pessimism would seem to be vindicated.

Yet his urbanism is not merely bleak and critical. The film's hope arises from its focuses on a salsa drumming group lead by Amadou for the hearing-impaired; the thunder of their unheard drums seems to float above the film, a mobilising motif that suggests another future beyond competition and fracture may be possible.

My second play at the Hampstead ended my residency with a chilling clarity. Press nights are bizarre affairs, with mood swings wilder than on a fever chart. Half the audience are scribbling while the other half try to cheer on the team. In these days when critics are replaced with the scattershot of Twitter, we forget their unexamined power back then. They too were hardly a model of diversity – almost exclusively male, middle-aged, mindful of their privileges, they descended on the theatre like an invading platoon, greeted by the press team who furnished them with free drinks, programmes and obeisance. The critics were mindful of their temporary power and exerted it without pity.

And in retrospect the play in question, *After the Gods*, was a doomed attempt to find laughs in the toxicity of contemporary universities and their lauding of 'Theory' – in this case with a central character, Michel de Beaudricourt, was based on the notorious case of Louis Althusser who murdered his wife in a fit of insanity, an act which seemed to reflect his brutally impersonal variant of Marxism. Not great material for comedy but the scattered and fitful responses to it on its opening night boded badly. Rehearsals had been rocky with the director falling ill and the theatre was distracted by its imminent move to a new building. Even so the work felt good and the cast were great. Yet at the interval I couldn't get the usually supportive Ben to endorse the play we'd all worked so hard on, and in the press for drinks I felt alone and exposed. And what was I playing at? What arrogance was this, imposing my in-jokes on this unimpressed smart set? London seemed to be there en masse, folding its arms and seeing through my pretensions.

The second half was no better; the audience had thinned out and the play seemed leaden and pedantic, long outstaying its welcome. The after-show party was grim, as the critics shot off to file their copy. How do you survive two successive flops, I thought, tipsy and sad on the train back to the blessed anonymity of Cambridge?

It was only the next day as the knocking copy landed that I discovered the night had been tragically overshadowed by the suicide of Simon Smith, my successor as Hampstead resident writer. Between the awestruck grief of the theatre staff at the news, the disengagement of the critics and the chastened actors working furiously to get a response, the play collapsed in real time, yielding a brutal suite of reviews. The fate of a show is trivial set against the loss of Simon's gift and life; but this was the end of my time in that version of Hampstead – maybe even my playwriting career – and felt like a portent of the darker decade to come.

12 *The Wind Will Carry Us*: Life during Wartime

(CAMBRIDGE, CAIRO, KYIV, GREELEY, SHEFFIELD, LEEDS)

EXT. MILL ROAD, CAMBRIDGE. AFTERNOON. 9.11.2001

I have a severe cold. I wander in search of a haircut; the barber winces as he trims my hair, his eyes are elsewhere.

I get home to where my son is wriggling on his nappy-mat. The phone rings. It's mum and dad, at the end of a long trip across America to mark their retirement. 'We're alright,' *mum shouts into the line.* 'Great,' *I answer, a little puzzled. Why would they not be?* 'We're staying about three blocks away but we're fine.' *The line is not good.*

'Turn on the television.'

CUT TO:

EXT. CAMBRIDGE TRAIN STATION. MORNING. 7.7.2005

Due to meet a famous director in London, I board the train, select my seat, sip my cappuccino. The departure time passes, the train remains static. Porters and staff run up and down the station. Passengers look up from lap-tops and phones and newspapers.

Minutes pass. We get restive. I angrily summon one of the station staff who whirls round and says, 'This train's not going anywhere mate.'

CUT TO:

EXT. TRAIN STATION, ALEXANDRIA, EASTERN UKRAINE. MORNING, SEPTEMBER 2005.

A year after the Orange Spring, the L'viv train sets me down on the empty platform; the town's a scene of desolation even Andrei Zyagintsev would flinch from. Every sign's in Cyrillic script; no one speaks English. I'm here on the trail of a Ukrainian gangmaster who inspired my play about migration Fast Labour *(2008). It's a hot September morning. I walk along the cracked concrete path to the town centre harried by dogs.*

CUT TO:

EXT. GREELEY, COLORADO, USA. EVENING, DECEMBER 2009.

A small town where Egyptian founder of radical Islamism Sayyid Qutb studied in 1949, subject of my play Ignorance/Jahilliyah *(2012). The temperature's twenty below. I have been advised not to go out but have stomped in thigh-high snow to the centre. Everything is shut with the exception of one Mexican diner.*

CUT TO:

EXT. TRAIN STATION, CAIRO, EGYPT. APRIL 2010. MORNING.

I jump on a train to a suburb where Qutb lived before dying in Nasser's prisons; the doors slam shut, the train moves off. I look around me: it's a female-only carriage. The women glare at me through their niqabs just as the men in the adjoining carriages glare through a partition window. I look down at the shifting floor, catch the eye of a little girl.

*

Life speeds up as we get older. The sustained episodes of the past reduce to a blur of events, like a time-lapse film or DVD on fast forward, mirroring the manic tempo of the new century buffeted by war and terror.

The decade of what Jason Burke calls *The 9/11 Wars* (2011) coincides with the birth of my two children, Joseph in 2000 and Miriam in 2004, my life as a playwright and work in universities. These separate lives run like parallel spools of film or the four frames of Mike Figgis's *Time Code* (2000). The slow time of home life, rearing young children with their pavement-crawling tempo, trudging to and from the school gates is spliced with writing my way into a world increasingly out of control and the complicated privilege of working in higher education.

Match cuts shift me from one person to another, days in one life butt up against those in another. I am in a library, I am in a playgroup, I am on a train to a theatre or a university. Here is everyday life, apparently locked into rhythms that seem to connect you to your own childhood; here's history, in wave after wave of new technology, backlashes to modernity, wars, politics unmoored from grounding truths. Where does playwriting sit in this maelstrom?

In a world of children, film-going acquires a newly heightened significance. As we hit the new millennium Hero's waters broke on Christmas Day as if in a Richard Curtis script. Joseph arrived blue and slippery, fist raised as if in a salute, extending his delivery and causing his mother a truly bloody labour. Her courage that day is not something I'll ever forget.

When I drove that terrifying parcel of humanity home from hospital, he seemed to fill the car with a quiet. We brought in his newly formed body curled in sleep, thumb plugged in; the house appeared to be the house of another person. Who allowed us to have this being in our home?

He sat in our living room, the street lit by drifts of snow, fascinated by his budding toes, the light from the bay window onto a quiet backstreet his first magic lantern show. I'd hold him up as if at the big screen and he'd gaze, like James Stewart in *Rear Window* (1954), piecing together the world from bin collectors, postal operatives and milk vans. That fixed camera position shot, one long stare, is his more benign version of the opening shot of Haneke's *Cache* (2005) or Victor Erice's steady gaze at a painter's canvas in *The Quince Tree Sun* (1992), as Antonio Lopez attempts to paint the eponymous tree.

With this child as absorbent as tissue on our living room floor, I couldn't bear anything cheap or crappy or cruel to be watched in his presence. This protective puritanism couldn't last long but I happened across the Humphrey Jennings's visionary film *A Diary for Timothy* (1946) with a war baby addressed by the patrician whisper of Michael Redgrave speaking E. M. Forster's script, gathering together '*the people of Britain'* in their various capacities – a miner, a farmer, Myra Hess performing in the National Gallery, John Gielgud hamming up Hamlet. The child's unfakeable reality calls out anything phoney, alongside this gallery of non-professionals, belying the propagandistic intent; here was a film fit for a newborn child.

The daze of early parenthood is a reset of life blurred by broken nights, time slowed down and stretched out all at once. Three years later Hero raised the question of a second child; I felt it might be a mistake. We'd achieved an equilibrium of sorts; why spoil that? Nine months later Miriam was born in giddying minutes as Hero and I prepared for a birthing pool, me standing by in swimmers.

Is love of cinema an inheritable trait? Or was taking our children to the cinema just another anachronistic gesture like walking in what remains of the countryside or training them away from sugar and carbs? Sugar and carbs of course are available aplenty in the world of family films from the urbane pleasures of Pixar (*Up* (2009), *Wall-E* (2008)) to endlessly rewatching DVDs of *Thomas and the Magic Railroad* (2000). Was it right to force the pace of them experiencing film as a kind of wonder and mystery too?

Quixotically I took them aged 9 and 5 to see Michelangelo Frammartino's *Le Quatro Volte* (2010). Many of the most significant films of our times are by artists like Frammartino, a cross-over film-maker moving from the gallery to the screen like Steve McQueen in his astonishing debut *Hunger* (2008), free from the demand to work to a conventional script, closer to documentary than drama. Frammartino's poem of a film puts its unscripted faith in the Pythagorean doctrine of metempsychosis showing the soul of an old man passing into a goat whose own death feeds the soil that contributes to fuel and fire. He offers a detached sense of life of as unwilled, appropriate to the muddle of parenting. As in all great stories for children, animals, trees and humans are here equivalent in interest.

Miriam was more gripped by Haifaa al-Mansour's moving fable of female subjection *Wadjda* (2012) documenting a girl two years her senior craving a pushbike in patriarchal Riyadh, the camera located at the level of the child, tracking her delimited journeys, caring about what she sees and cares for. The warm quotidian reality of the film gives the lie to the '*Two Civilizations'* hypothesis driving the Global War on Terrorism, al-Mansour courageously reclaiming artistic space, directing by way of a monitor in the back of a van to avoid contact with the male crew, subverting that zero-sum analysis.

These films were simply an extension of the bay window where we'd hold up the children to gaze at the world – there, look at that, be amazed by it, understand it as part of your world. And in the first decade of the twenty-first century this was more necessary than ever before; first, because the world had accelerated into a new interlinked reality with the panopticon of the Internet. Secondly, because that daily global collision emerged countering shock waves – mass migration, the eruption of terror, reckless wars unleashed by the US and supported by our leaders. Film – and theatre – served to resist the flow of images and ideology.

In the theatre this provoked an instant rethink; suddenly the 1990s' tiny concerns with the pleasures of Ecstasy and the dilemmas of flat-sharing looked ill-suited to this new world of a thousand unnatural shocks.

The immediate artistic response was to disavow fiction altogether, refashioning the stage as a place of documentation through so-called Verbatim plays. The movement has roots in German theatre in the 1920s and 1960s, but had its first resurgence in the America of the 1990s with the courageous ventures of the actor Anna Deavere Smith into the polarised wreckage of riot-torn New York and LA in *Fires in the Mirror* (1992) or *Twilight: Los Angeles, 1992* (1994), or Moises Kaufmann's humanist investigation of the homophobic murder of Matthew Shepard in Laramie, Wyoming in 1998, *The Laramie Project* (2000). Both 'plays' entered into the breach where the documentary work of D. A. Pennebaker or Fred Wiseman might have gone, forensically dissecting two tragedies for the deeper insight of the audience. In the UK after 9/11 suddenly we had the work of the Tricycle Theatre in Kilburn under its director Nick Kent staging '*tribunal plays*' such as *The Colour of Justice* (1999), which re-enacted the inquiry into the inept and racist handling of the murder of African-Caribbean teenager Stephen Lawrence in 1993; or *Guantanamo* (2004) which assembled testimony from British-born prisoners '*rendered*' into the US's extralegal internment camp. It seemed life moved too fast for fictional treatment; that theatre needed to optimise its role as first responder, capitalise on its topical powers, be literally '*news that stays news*', to quote Ezra Pound.

And this work had a galvanising effect on all of us who practised fiction. It certainly informed my next play *World Music* which I consider my proper debut, opening at Sheffield's Crucible Theatre in 2003, where my first serious theatre viewing took place, before transferring down to the Donmar Warehouse in London the following year.

The play came out of my faltering attempts to support the work of Oxfam or the World Development Movement, hubristically seeking somehow to atone for our colonial past. Much of the late 90s was given over to the politics of resistance to globalisation and the indebted state of the Global South, with movements like the World Social Forum inspired by writers such as Naomi Klein, critiquing corporations and North–South inequities. I'd become friends with writer Matthew Carr who'd author a counter-history of terrorism (*The Infernal Machine* (2010)) and document the refugee crisis provoked by the War on Terror (*Fortress Europe* (2012)). Our conversations gave me the courage to place my own writing in a more international and political context.

I wanted to address the notion of the '*International community*' cruelly exposed by our calamitous responses to the Balkan wars or the Rwandan genocide in 1994. The West's confused reaction to those horrific events seemed clouded by neocolonial guilt, with France charging in disingenuously and Britain, the US and the United Nations all failing to stop the state-sanctioned slaughter of the Tutsi minority by the Hutu majority. I sought out Rwandan émigrés living in the UK, tracing a community in West London living in the wake of trauma, guided by a woman called Mary whose brother had been one of those murdered. She brought me into the community of survivors, gathering each year in April at the Brompton Oratory to mark their unimaginable losses in ceremonies of quiet grace. I edited their testimonies which defied invention and wondered what exactly my fiction could add.

Feeling this was a story about Europe and its shared past, not just the UK, I set the action in the European Parliament in Brussels, capital of one of the most brutal colonial powers in Central Africa; the ironies of this temple of cooperation towering over a city built on slave labour and genocide was too potent to overlook. I shadowed my regional MEP at work there, sharing free and fancy lunches at which he was relentlessly lobbied by interest groups. The airless world of the European Parliament, its closed committees where trade deals were hammered out, its vast chambers where speakers droned through the imminent new constitution seemed so divorced from any democratic foundations as to defy his attempt to keep things real. By 2000 I had a draft which got dusty answers from most theatres and was passed on by the Hampstead; but after 9/11 things changed and it reached Michael Grandage, a former actor now making his name as a director and producer, turning the Crucible in Sheffield into one of the UK's most exciting venues.

Michael, a generous and brilliant impresario, matched me with a new director, young Salford-born Cambridge graduate Josie Rourke, then 22. Rourke's meticulously assembled production, mounted on the thrust stage of the Crucible, was fleeting but defined my sense of the theatre I dreamed of: epic yet intimate, critical yet emotional. Among its cast assembled with great care by one of my former students Amy Ball was a rainbow of actors who would go on to define the decade: Nikki Amuka-Bird (astonishing), Nigel Lindsay (Islamist convert in Chris Morris's wickedly funny *Four Lions* (2010)), Paul Ready, Sara Powell, Sebastian Harcombe, the massive young British-Nigerian Nonso Anozie and Madagascan Assly Zandry. The multiculturalism or interculturalism of the company itself was as thrilling as it was rare.

The play's form echoed the film I had consumed, offering a theatrical equivalent to Roeg's asynchronous splicing of time and place, crossing continents and decades before settling to a final deadly reckoning with that past, and all evoked on Christopher Oram's elegantly minimal space, lit by Neil Austin's open lights and given sonic form in Gareth Fry's sound design. I know the play could be critiqued for its reach for allegory, for its potentially reductive reading of African realities, for its sheer presumption; but I felt I'd created a new kind of narrative worth those risks.

I sat apprehensively in the vast amphitheatre of the Crucible, a 900-seater, audience on three sides, with entries from so-called vomitoria on four sides enabling a sweep of movement and flow of events. The show was a loss-leader, post-snooker season, but as the lights dimmed and the actors filled the space, the shared charge in the audience was palpable; I could sense the people of Sheffield leaning in together to follow this continent-crossing story. Mary, beside me on opening night, had to be talked down at the interval from her rage at the character of Jean, a genocidaire in the play, whom she took to be real; she wanted to confront him there and then and I had to clarify to her this was only in fact a fiction. Her reaction humbled me; what exactly was I doing with this play?

My emergence as a playwright had been stymied by shortcomings in craft. I had little awareness of how to work with audiences, something that can only be learned sitting among them, gauging their chart of feeling. I had to learn what the carrying capacity of the stage might offer relative to the screen and the first act's payload of nearly twenty scenes, some short as a minute, pushed the production to the limits of comprehension. Yet in Rourke's hands the assembled company created a kind of choreographic temporal-spatial blur that lucidly enacted its logic. If my work at the Hampstead had been a false start, that first run in Sheffield during a hot June is one of the highlights of my career.

Equally there was the pleasure of working in a great regional city, a pleasure repeated when working in 2008 at the West Yorkshire Playhouse in Leeds on *Fast Labour* or the Birmingham Repertory Theatre on *Europa* (2013). With the acting company away from home, the city's bars and restaurants become a shared hub of conversation, the thin sociology of London theatre offset by a less self-aware audience and to be frank, a less bourgeois one. Likewise, the theatre staff are part of a continuum with the civic life of the city. Sheffield and Leeds were both experiencing that uplift and growth of the Blair years, reinventing themselves as cultural hubs.

But how did cinema respond to this '*low dishonest decade*'? It's notable the first responders were documentaries or docudramas; Michael Moore unleashed his incendiary *Fahrenheit 9/11* in 2004, eschewing subtlety for confrontation and conspiracy. Michael Winterbottom's documentary-inflected approach enabled him to craft his moving account of migration *In This World* (2002) and incarceration in *The Road to Guantanamo* (2006), films as sharp as a charcoal sketch. Equally important was the work of TV directors such as Peter Kosminsky (*The Government Inspector* (2005) and *Britz* (2007)) or Nick Broomfield's *Battle for Haditha* (2007) or anything by Adam Curtis. Mainstream Hollywood had little to offer other than the fetishistic procedural work of Katherine Bigelow in *The Hurt Locker* (2008) and *Zero Dark Thirty* (2012). Yet the '*forever wars*' which kept journalists and writers at bay seemed hard to penetrate except through the lens of the sufferings of American servicemen and women.

Cinema does not move fast by and large; only Winterbottom's rapid tempo of production, emulating Fassbinder, kept pace with headlong events. Film and topicality are rare bedfellows in the way theatre enters its own. Equally since the abolition of censorship in 1968, theatre, a low-capital form, is freer than either film or TV in its room for manoeuvre even if it is constrained in reach. But it was the film-making of the Muslim and Arabic world that proved most essential in pushing back on narratives of the neoconservatives and their fellow travellers.

I've already mentioned Saudi Arabian film; Elia Suleiman produced a series of wry essayistic films examining Palestinian experience in quietly angry films such as *The Time That Remains* (2008). Further north, in the increasingly Islamicised Turkey, the emergence of Nuri Bilge Ceylan offered a sense, as his fellow countryman Orhan Pamuk's novels do, of a culture on the cusp of West and East, able to see beyond those antinomies. *Uzak* (2002), his breakthrough film, shifts between the rural interior and the vast sprawl of Istanbul, with two cousins forming the film's odd couple shot in his own flat. It's often funny, with a wonderful joke about Mahmut, a middle-class photographer, masking his porn with a 'viewing' of *Stalker*. The film's attention to lives lived between ideologies and caught in puzzlement is recognisable to anyone who might have seen Chabrol's *Les Cousins* (1959) or Billy Wilder's *The Apartment* (1960).

Ceylan steers clear of direct commentary on the conflicts that encircle Turkey but offers wry insights into their source. His greatest film *Once Upon a Time in Anatolia* (2011) unfolds at a serpentine pace, the camera so far back that the car it shows winding through treeless plains becomes an insect in a sea of steppe; yet in it sits a murderer, a medic and a cop, all seeking an elusive corpse in a world of little justice and less reason. Villages emptied by migration are blighted by crimes of ignorance and poverty on the Anatolian plain that defines and divides Eurasia. Its regional importance is evident in Jafar Panahi's allusion to it in his *Tehran Taxi* (2015), made in direct defiance of the 20-year ban the Iranian state had imposed on him, where we see *Once Upon a Time . . .* among the pirated DVDs circulated by a spiv. Ceylan's most recent films, *Winter Sleep* (2014) and *The Wild Pear Tree* (2018), assert their shared ancestry with Chekhov, another master of provincial life, the former restaging *Uncle Vanya* in the weird troglodyte dwellings of Cappadoccia, the latter hymning a lost generation of overeducated young men, caught between the city and the region, drawn to mysticism and evading the call-up to police the country's eastern badlands. While Ceylan rarely directly confronts Islamist radicalisation, the conditions he films with such humanity might have turned the head of a nineteenth-century Russian nihilist towards political terror.

Iran is of course neither Arabic nor the apparent target of the Global War on Terrorism; nevertheless, with its rich culture of film, it is the main chronicler of life within the Islamic world. Take Mohsen Makhmalbaf's astonishing *Kandahar* (2001) which explores the Talibanisation of Iran's northern neighbour, Afghanistan, by tracking a Canadian émigré's return in full burqa to trace her sister. That same courageous feminism is equally evident in the work of his daughter Samira whose 1998 debut *The Apple* was made when she was 17, going on in her follow-up, *Blackboards* (2000), to track the Kurdish victims of Saddam Hussein, as does the Kurdish-made *A Time for Drunken Horses* (2000), viscerally shot by Bahman Ghobad on the mountainous borders of Iraq and Iran. Fusing Persian lyricism with a tough neorealism that much of the world had set aside, these films unlock and humanise the apparently impenetrable Middle East we were encouraged to see as our enemy.

I watched them while teaching Drama at Homerton College on Cambridge's fringe, my first gig in higher education. In this enclave of teachers turned academics, coffee was served in the common room at 11 a.m. by an unsmiling woman with auburn hair. The coffee was dire, but it was the only coffee available and if you turned up later than 11.15 it was no longer available. As I was always turning up at about 11.17, I found myself at the sharp end of this rigorous system, discovering that my nemesis was herself Iranian. One morning, late again, the coffee whisked away, I mentioned *A Time for Drunken Horses*. Had my nemesis seen it? After the initial confusion, her face melted; yes, yes, she'd certainly seen it. Not only that, she'd seen *The Apple,* she'd seen *Taste of Cherry*, she'd seen *Blackboards*, she'd seen *The Wind Will Carry Us*. For her these were not obscure art-house films but despatches from a country she was exiled from; her eyes filled with tears as she spoke of her family still there, near the Iraqi border, as the drumbeats of the American invasion grew ever louder.

Behind all these films lies the luminous example of director Abbas Kiarostami. He learned his craft under the Shah in the 1970s, but refused exile under Khomeini, fashioning instead an increasingly oblique body of films, at times as simple and profound as a sketch by Paul Klee. His best work precedes the insanity of the 9/11 decade but stands in resistance to it; one of the first shocks of the culture wars was America's refusal in 2001 to issue him a visa to enter the US as his last celluloid film worked its way around the world. I'd got to know him through *Close-Up* (1990) and his most austere film *Taste of Cherry* (1997), a leisurely road movie, its Everyman a suicidal motorist circling Tehran and the characters he picks up to assist him in his own death, a Kurd, an Afghan and an Azeri, allegories of the region's fault lines. You can almost smell the heaps of burning rubbish in the dusk, see the smog laid out over the city, feel the waning heat of the sun; the slurring of tyres on gravel as the car rounds another switchback is the only soundtrack. Buried in the sparseness of the images and the plotless action is a sceptical philosophy outlining the limits of human will; even this terminal task requires the kindness of strangers. The lone driver uncovers other isolated lives in his quest and his journey is not simply geographical, it's a *via negativa* away from society, a peeling away of the layers of life.

Kiarostami's next film, *The Wind Will Carry Us* (1999), offered an even more enigmatic riposte to the arrogance of the coming decade which would see Tony Blair parading his newly acquired expertise in Shi'ism or Whitehouse aides peddling destructive regional clichés as cover for military aggression. Any film with 'wind' in the title from *Gone with the Wind* (1939) to Taiwanese master Hou Hsiao-hsien's *Dust in the Wind* (1986) emphasises the centrality of fate and chance in our lives. The destructive chaos of the 9/11 decade arose from the reasserted trumph of the will in resurgent neoconservativism and its hubristic dreams of the West reshaping the world through military intervention, Iraq as their bloody chessboard.

Kiarostami's fable takes the form of another road movie into the golden northern lands of Iran. The setting is a remote village tunnelled into rock like a beehive, its maze of streets curving into themselves, its troglodyte houses bedecked with the bright shocks of carpets. At one point an apple rolls its way down from an off-kilter shelf and leads the protagonist (if that is the right word), an Engineer, into the village's inner organs, where, in a cave-like cellar, he finds a young woman milking a cow. She recites a poem by Forough Farrokhzad, a female Iranian poet and film-maker who died tragically young, thereby glossing the film's elliptical title: '*The wind will carry us / the wind will carry us*.' The Engineer's looming yet irrelevant presence, the woman milking the cow in the half-light, indifferent to his gaze, embody the hermetic power of this film which took me back to my own journeys into the Anatolian interior.

In Kiarostami's film the touristic desire to look and to appropriate is everywhere refuted; each act of communication falls short; as Paul Theroux noted, '*the tourist doesn't know where he has been, the traveller doesn't know where he is going*.' The Engineer, who we know as little of as the villagers, attempts to reach Tehran with his hopeless mobile phone, driving up to the wind-blown cemetery to gain a signal and foolishly berating his intermittent interlocutor. Gradually he loses all purpose and the film drifts into a different temporal logic, as he's swallowed in the mystery of the village and the fate of a hidden people that refuses to yield its secrets to hasty visitants. Kiarostami's golden-hued film obeys the same logic, embodying his commitment to a, '*half-created cinema, an unfinished cinema which attains completion through the creative spirit of the audience*'.

The first decade of this century took too little care of such mysteries; the Kurds wherever they are distributed remain oppressed even as they have been chief among the forces resisting the worst of Saddam's Baathism or the insane project of ISIS. Kiarostami's film is not an ethnographic account of a 'people'; it has too much tact and acknowledges the limits of cinema and indeed of art. I've never had the good fortune to visit Iran; years later I wrote a drama for the BBC World Service about the events around the fall of the Shah in 1979 but was frustrated in obtaining a visa. But I was lucky enough to talk to some of the most formidable Iranian émigrés such as human rights lawyer Shirin Ebadi. In her example and indeed the films of Kiarostami and his successor Asghar Farhadi, whose masterpiece *A Separation* (2010) gave great courage to his nation when it was awarded Best Foreign Film at the Oscars, true resistance is apparent. The work of these artists and activists is a testimony to a world that resists categorisation and offers a standing reproach to the West's desire to dominate what eludes its grasp.

Yet this decade, my entry into those confusing middle years of life, only confirmed I was not the master of my own destiny: the imperatives of children; the imperatives of work pulling me in every direction; the imperatives of history in its crazy trajectories all giving the lie to the '*active protagonists*' with '*clear objectives*' called for in mainstream drama. The very notion of the hero's journey seemed as much symptom of a world locked in intractable conflict as a solution. It was time to create a kind of writing that put human activity in its place in a world we were making increasingly uninhabitable.

13 *An Inconvenient Truth*: Green Screens

(IMPINGTON)

INT. A VILLAGE HALL IN IMPINGTON, CAMBRIDGESHIRE.
NIGHT.

Chairs scrape and camping tables are shifted to accommodate tea urns. A crowd of villagers settle on hard chairs to watch a film.

In 2002 we moved north of Cambridge, the wrong side of the A14, and into Middle England.

The ring of villages that surround the city, once declining rural settlements, are now suburbs where scientists, cycling in lycra to the Cambridge Science Park, rub shoulders with artisans and pensioners. These '*fen edge*' villages have few farmers in them nor recognisable fens – and what farming takes place is intensive and science-driven. It's a landscape of flat fields under vast skies, new towns erupting out of black soil, its shrinking peat bearing witness to what's been displaced, preserved in embattled pockets such as nearby Wicken Fen reserve.

Impington is the stage set for my middle age and the children's education; blurring into neighbouring Histon, this is a planned settlement designed to serve the local Chivers landowners and their huge fruit orchards. Low Church by inclination their jam factory battened onto the railway line, now serving a guided bus transport system. Villagers live in the legacy of agriculture, industry and model accommodation, our garden graced with remnant apple trees, ghosts of lost orchards, our older neighbours former packers and pickers. Local houses, the doctor's surgery, the churches share the same late Victorian vintage and speak to a visionary sense of a Garden England; indeed the secondary school our kids attend opened in 1939, designed by exiled modernist architect Walter Gropius, his only completed building during his short tenure in the country. This convergence of modernism and rurality makes being in Impington like living in a documentary from the GPO Unit in the 1930s, or a drawing by Eric Ravilious.

It's also like so much of the world under threat given that much of the land that stretches down from the gouged-out waist of the Wash is below or at sea level, with some maps showing projected sea-level rises in the next hundred years bringing the coast to our neighbouring village Cottenham. These reclaimed lands, drained in the seventeenth century, are always at risk of returning to their watery origins. Perhaps that's why, with local residents working in conservation or for organisations such as the British Antarctic Survey, we find ourselves in a crowded Baptist church for a screening of Al Gore's 2006 docu-lecture *An Inconvenient Truth*, a film designed to disseminate swiftly, to be projected in community halls, schools and churches, places people gather and begin to talk to each other.

It's a truism that film is primarily a form of entertainment and filmed lectures are clearly a long way from entertainment; but some films change the world, and this is one of them. In it Gore cuts a reassuring figure making light work of the climate science. The director Davis Guggenheim doesn't get in the way, works in some hokey cutaways to Gore wandering his tobacco plantations in the golden light that's obligatory when celebrating American life (*'Learning it from your dad on the farm. That's something special'*). These interludes may be dull, but they buffer the devastating facts of anthropogenic climate change elsewhere. The text is chummy and insiderish; Gore knows everyone, Charles Keeling, Carl Sagan. But given a film this anodyne still elicited challenges to stop it being shown in schools, such flourishes are forgivable. Because Gore takes upon himself the role of a doctor delivering the very worst diagnosis to the world and this requires an amiable bedside manner. By the time he reprises the images of Earth Rise which commences the film with the caption *'our only home'*, offering the rallying cry, *'It is time to rise up and procure our future'*, all doubts melt away. Gore's *'mission to explain'* and his personal stations of the cross illuminate the way ahead; for an hour at least.

Our screening is well-attended; 300 or so people out of a village of 8,000 make their way into the large Victorian hall on the basis of a poster wrapped illegally around lamp posts. As film enters the community, screened in a place that's familiar and valued, its reach is double any skim on a small screen. When the lights come up and tea urns are wheeled out, the event becomes a town-hall meeting. Neighbours articulate their fears: the faulty drainage systems in the village; the threat to the green belt by new housing; the air pollution from the local trunk road. Out of this clamour arises something that can't be called a movement but surely is unprecedented: a community carbon reduction group, which we call HICCA (Histon and Impington Climate Change Action). What that amounts to is a bunch of geologists, climatologists, conservationists, pensioners and parents meeting in our kitchen and planning, well, other meetings. Events. The founding of a community orchard. My children will never forgive us for making them join a Feast Parade dressed as carbon or blued up like Gaia shouting *'Reduce, Reuse, Recycle'*.

And more film screenings: *Age of Stupid* (2009) by Franny Armstrong (which Philip French described as a *'hecture'*, a cross between a lecture and a hector), *Home* (2009) by aerial photographer Yann Arthus-Bertrand (after an hour of shots of devastation Glenn Close, the narrator, blithely states, *'It's too late for pessimism'*), *The Power of Community: How Cuba Survived Peak Oil* (2006) – or presentations by beekeepers, writers such as Mark Lynas, government scientists such as the late David MacKay. As a scientifically illiterate writer I found myself trying to thrash out plans for the community. Can we agree to mobilise around keeping average temperature rises below 2 degrees? Oh no, says one Antarctic scientist, far too broad-brush. One of our number, an American, is chastening in his intensity, girding us on to more action, demanding we hold '*house church*' meetings, roll out cheap solar panels. Given we have kids and jobs and lives, the demands become overwhelming and the truculent mystification of some of our neighbours dispiriting. Even getting the speed limit down to 20 mph seems beyond the police. But if we don't do something, will anyone else?

The '*deficit model*' of communicating science, rooted in the notion that simply telling the public the facts will elicit action, proves insufficient. Is it that the problem of climate change is so enormous that we struggle to envisage it? The ecological thinker Timothy Morton has called it a '*hyper-object*'. The group withers a little, people drift away and daily more and more carbon is deposited in the atmosphere.

In 2008 all this activity provoked a new play from me, one that would lead me into the world of film. I embarked on a commission for the Bush Theatre where my old comrade Josie Rourke was now artistic director. The theatre building itself, a space over a pub facing onto Shepherd's Bush roundabout, had taken a direct hit when it was flooded in the unprecedented rainfall that saturated the UK in 2007. A theatre whose very wiring was now disabled needed less encouragement in confronting the future but it's surprising to reflect now how few theatres did recognise any such necessity back then. Given our own house had been flooded in one hour of psychotic rain that seemed to make the air sheer water, climate chaos, as it was becoming branded, was no longer a theoretical concern; yet how could its story be felt as well as told?

This acceleration of concern about climate was for me part of a larger question about our dire ecological impact on the biosphere. Film in some ways is ideally placed to ask such questions given its commitment to place, to the drama of humans and environment. The major genres are defined by landscape – the western foremost among them, sci-fi likewise – in a way that theatre, a more human and socially focused form, is not. And science fiction's commitment to chastening futures was proving to be the go-to mode of representation, whether in the noisy mode of the rebooted disaster movie (*The Day After Tomorrow* (2004)) or in resurgent post-apocalyptica such as John Hillcoat's *The Road* (2009)). But disaster movies simply fetishise catastrophe, relish it as a suitable challenge for their CGI team to conjure up spectacles worthy of the Victorian painter John 'Mad' Martin; humans become mere fodder for a diorama of destruction. Apocalyptica is surely only the western or the romance by other means, with Cormac MacCarthy's sober dread played out as a bleak variant of *Lord of the Rings*, Viggo Mortensen cast to ensure the connection – if all that's left to do is survive, there's little left to be done.

How can drama register the complexity of nature and resituate us among it in a way that's not just about horror? The example of Werner Herzog is useful given he reframes the human story within a wider set of determinations, whether Fitzcarraldo hacking his way through the Amazon or Kasper Hauser positioned between nature and society. Herzog's documentaries from *Grizzly Man* (2005) to *Encounters at the End of the World* (2007) relentlessly investigate that boundary, revealing the known world to be as paradoxical as anything in sci-fi. Or Terrence Malick's early films, in particular *Days of Heaven* (1978),which view their protagonists as flora and fauna in the American landscape as if he were cinema's Thoreau. Did Malick's study of Heidegger inform his desire in this film to get his cinematographers Nestor Almendros and Haskell Wexler to deploy natural light at all costs? Either way he framed the shooting schedule around the weather with much of it taking place in the '*magic hour*' as dusk commenced. That reverence for place and time deepens his critique of the heroic westward migration American story, presenting it instead as an act of headlong internal colonialism, with the lonely figure of farmer Sam Shepard embodying its futility. Time and again the film's central romance – Richard Gere, Brooke Adams, Shepard – is set aside for the contemplation of a locust or a character's death viewed from a riverbed.

Malick's ecological concerns resurface in the films of Kelly Reichardt, a film-maker firmly located in the north-west, who also subtly dissects colonising narratives. In her fabulously spare western *Meek's Cut-Off* (2010) or her eco-thriller *Night Moves* (2013), the landscape becomes the core of the drama; in the latter a dam, in the former relentlessly dry plains, which put human life in a hydrological context. As the great Jean Renoir said, '*I cannot conceive of a cinema without water*.' Malick's spirit also animates the deeply located films of Debra Granik and Anne Rossellini, whether in their debut *Winter's Bone* (2010) or the deeply moving *Leave No Trace* (2017) which captures the aboriginal old-growth forests of Oregon now so ravaged by fire.

Yet theatre takes place in a human landscape, the controlled realm of the stage under artificial light; and my venue, the Bush, was then a small space accommodating sixty people served by a tiny dressing room. My original idea of a drama that jumped between the corridors of power in Whitehall and a remote coastal setting in Norfolk as both experience an unprecedented coastal flood, was not realisable under such constraints. Josie gave me the courage to split the plays into two, thereby forming the diptych *The Contingency Plan*. *On the Beach*, set on the marshes of North Norfolk, explores the flood's tragic impact on a family of a glaciologist father and son – characters directly drawn from my neighbours. *Resilience*, a nightmarish political farce in Whitehall, watches the son enter the bear pit of politics in the heat of the flood crisis. Both plays mapped onto each other and adopted long real-time scenes as a way of disarming audience scepticism and releasing the cast – Robin Soans, Susan Brown, Stephanie Street, Geoff Streatfield and David Bark-Jones – to dictate the tempo of the evening or indeed the day when they played the show as a double bill.

So much of this show felt unprecedented and utopian: the luxury of two interlocking plays, with the story hanging somewhere between them, the largesse of having a team of two directors (Mike Longhurst and Tamara Harvey) sharing one designer (Tom Scutt) and a common cast. Mike Bradwell, the previous artistic director of the Bush, described it as a '*place where it was impossible to lie*' and its immersive naturalism ensured the story got under the defences of audiences unconvinced that my '*near-future*' scenario was imminent. The day of the press night was extended over six hours with supper in between; the theatre was half full of critics packed in a phalanx of scepticism either about my work and/or the themes of the play. Yet as it unfolded, I could sense things shifting and changing and even a palpable shock in the house. That night I slept fitfully in Josie's flat across from the theatre; she woke me with pastries and the overnight reviews. It seemed we'd hit our target. I still relish the musings of Charles Spencer, theatre critic of climate-change sceptic newspaper the *Daily Telegraph*, who spent much of his review rehearsing his resistance to the play's thesis before succumbing to what he called '*a theatrical knockout*'.

Theatre's reach exceeds its grasp; after a two-month packed-out run in front of 3,000 people, the chatter and interest in the plays have continued to this moment. The noise around the play alerted interest in other media for a potential adaptation and I found myself meeting the head of development for Film 4 and then production companies whom I – I! - would choose to help me develop the script. I felt a misplaced dizzy sense of power as I waltzed into the office of Michael Winterbottom's Revolution Films near King's Cross, its almost comically cool interior fitted out with deep sofas where supplicants sink in embarrassment as the 'team' hang out to quiz you – bikes dangled from the ceiling, the man himself looming over the edit of his horrifically violent *The Killer Inside Me* (2010). I sensed I'd be stuck in a queue there so opted to work instead with Cowboy Films, a equally funky small outfit who'd produced the film of *The Last King of Scotland* (2006) and the TV drama *Top Boy* (2011). Impressed by their commitment to the script, I embarked on a pyrrhic journey to the screen.

Another playwright had warned me the average timeline of script to green light took seven years; but while I was handsomely rewarded, what was most painful in this process was the slippage from my writing something unprecedented to my writing something all too familiar. The impact of the play(s) lay in their engagement with the unseen – the maritime floods that define their action remain offstage; the landscapes they inhabit are imagined not shown. This suggestiveness, not to mention long scenes of debate, was not what anyone wanted to see on-screen, even though for me, the best transpositions of plays to film retain and proclaim their origin: Louis Malle's *My Dinner with Andre* (1981) or *Vanya on 42nd Street* (1994); Barry Jenkins's *Moonlight* (2016), which in its fictional meditation on playwright Tarrell Alvin McCraney's childhood Miami, retaining an act structure and long real-time scenes with the intensity of theatre. Likewise, by collapsing the two plays into one drama some of the strangeness of the story was lost and I found myself too often reaching for tired tropes of political thrillers. In attempting to fill out the story, the body of the play shrunk to accommodate less well-founded scenes and realities. Even the preliminary process of poring over '*beat sheets*' and plot points, in the prescriptive fashion governing screenwriting, felt inimical. Writing is an existential act; how can I predict where a character will be in the final moments if I haven't discovered all the intervening ones? Still I was being well-paid and I was new on the block, so I strapped in and did what I was told.

This process of slippage only accelerated when we finally got a director on board. He was a talented young gun who'd cut his teeth on a trendy TV show I'd missed; I was relaxed with the notion that he'd need his say and sway. We went for a pub lunch to hammer out some ideas. What were we watching? Pretentiously perhaps, I offered Bergman's *Shame* (1968) as a reference point for the film's tone; the director, a film-school grad, hadn't seen it and didn't seem keen to do so – he suggested one of the Bourne franchise movies. OK, I hadn't seen it and wasn't keen to either, but I dutifully watched it and quite enjoyed it, all the time wondering what bearing it had on my play. Fine, it was a thriller. We needed more jeopardy; so climate change doesn't provide that? We need to '*open things up*'; the story's too localised, too British. We need to '*punch it up*', add in '*plate shots*', so we can cut away to, say, New York or some Caribbean island to widen the story's appeal. I tried out all of this; civil servants became hack journalists, the flood took place in a nuclear power station with one of the characters D-locked to the foundations; yes, it all had to be a conspiracy, scientists had to die, probably murdered. How's that for jeopardy?

Let's do another draft.

I got a call, late at night, after the tenth or so draft. The director seemed to like it – phew! But there was one small thing he wanted to see in the next draft: can we open the film in a desert? I was puzzled – why open in a desert when the story's set in the UK? And which particular desert did he have in mind? He didn't really know, he just wanted the film to open in a desert. '*It's a visual thing.*' OK. But doesn't a '*visual thing*' need to arise from the story? In truth, I was too acquiescent to say that, I simply feigned excited agreement – cool, a desert, let's go! – and rang off and contrived a way to deliver it. Cowboy were none too happy to see their budget suddenly spike; the '*visual thing*' got quietly cut in draft number eleven. And then, as I suspected he always would, the director made his excuses, Hollywood was calling and the script bounced back ending up on the slush pile where it's remained.

The fate of my adaptation is hardly unusual and I take full responsibility for the outcome; this partisan version is not to be trusted. Even so there's a deeper moral here about the relationship between writing plays and films which is something I debate in seminar rooms and attempted to touch on in my book *The Secret Life of Plays* (2010). One of the most insightful commentaries on the role of the screenwriter in film-making comes from Jean-Claude Carrière in his *The Secret Language of Film* (1994). Given Carrière worked with everyone from Luis Bunuel to Michael Haneke, his observations carry more weight than the plethora of diktats issues by screenwriting gurus from Syd Field to Robert McKee. Carrière talks of the '*vanishing screenplay*': '*Once the film exists, the screenplay is no more.*' He speaks of his first engagement with film working with the legendary Jacques Tati who delegated his tuition in the craft to his editor, the equally legendary Suzanne Baron. Placing a screenplay next to her editing suite and spooling the resulting film back and forth, she puts her hand on the script and says: '*The whole problem is to get from this to this.*' For Carrière the script is a larval form, like the casing of a butterfly, discarded once it is ready to fly. It is read by no one other than the collaborators and has no literary stature; yet it is critical to the film's success. It's an insight all would-be screenwriters know in their heart.

But a sense of a common endeavour and equal weighting is surely the precondition of any collaboration; in theatre, this is generally a given. In film it seems too often not to be so; but if it is to be, the touchstone, the reference point behind that collaboration is surely the reality spoken of in the film as much as cinema's own prehistory. At no point did my director express any interest in the questions that animated my plays about the climate crisis, as if doing so was a vulgarity or my crankish concern. His reference points were simply other films that reminded him of my story; and my task was to make my story look like those other films. When that was achieved everything interesting in my story was gone, the script was hollow and impersonal. This might offer some explanation as to why so many films feel so predictable in their thrust, dependent on steroidal injections of CGI or technique to mask their core banality. And why the best films still often seem to be the product of directors who see themselves as auteurs. It certainly has enhanced my admiration for the work of screenwriters who survive and resist the dilution of their work.

My experience was hardly unique; I had a good time working with Cowboy who were supportive throughout. I downloaded Final Draft. I got a whiff of the business. I attended a Film 4 pre-Cannes drinks party as if I myself was pre-Cannes. And slowly the project dwindled away. Yet the play survives and gave courage to a generation of climate-change plays: *Earthquakes in London* (2010), *Lungs* (2011). Theatre no longer disavows this question as one that couldn't be dramatised.

The problem of telling the story of climate change is a minor one compared to the problem of addressing the catastrophe of climate change. I consider all of my work to be in some sense environmentally focused; for that reason, film offers an enduring example to theatre and other media. Yet beyond documentary, film has barely begun to find a way into this, the greatest challenge we face.

Back in Impington, after three years of stop-start community activism, HICCA fractured. After 2010 the Tory-led coalition government steadily reneged on their '*greenest government ever*' commitments and the toxic community of denialism migrated into the new outlets of virulent populism. The world is on fire, sometimes literally, and any art that cannot acknowledge and engage with that is part of the problem not the solution.

Our orchard has thrived though, replanted with apple varieties on the verge of extinction, a habitat to a myriad of insects and birds. Without Al Gore's film this home to jays and brimstone butterflies might well have been a new housing estate.

(BRISTOL, CAMBRIDGE, NORWICH)

EXT. THE RIVER AVON, HAM GREEN. MORNING.
At the edge of farmland, a hard-earth path opens up to the vista of a muddy brown river curving its way towards Bristol.

2016 was a difficult year – personally and politically.

I'd turned 50 and had my greatest success yet with my play *Temple* (2015) at the Donmar Warehouse. Everything in this process was a delight to me. I was working with Simon Russell Beale, the finest stage actor of his generation, whose wry, ironic inflections navigated my lines in a way that has reverberated ever since. The director was Howard Davies, whose intensity of attention enabled a production of sure-footed truth; to watch Howard squeezing Blu-Tack in his hands, his blue eyes tracking the actors' work, shifting their decisions with a conductor's briskness, was a joy. The play, dramatising the travails of St Paul's Cathedral as it negotiated the Occupy demonstration of 2011, epitomised the sort of theatre I'd become committed to: comic, precise, political, a close gaze at a closed world. It sold out, received great reviews and the Donmar, a super-stylish venue with its rehearsal rooms in Dryden Street, felt like a home from home. I was all set to work with Howard again, no inkling that within a year he'd die of cancer.

That Christmas I succumbed to a terrible infection, retreating to bed shivering, a ball of pain burning my guts; a stomach bug? A virus? Despite early infirmity I've enjoyed good health all my life, I'd no script for the precarity that followed. On Christmas Day Hero drove me to hospital, limping and wincing into A & E. The surgeon in tinsel-adorned scrubs announced I'd have to have a catheter fitted – as he left the curtained-off room, I looked in panic at Hero. Was a catheter fitted through the penis or the stomach? Reassuringly as the daughter of a doctor, she thought the latter. But in this instance, she was wrong.

Hours later I was in a ward high over the bare fields of Cambridgeshire during a winter that never happened, diagnosed with near-fatal sepsis and on drips and feeds galore. I protected myself by bingeing on film. Everything I watched seared into me: *The Imitation Game* (2014) which I'd shunned as a gung-ho biopic with a show-off turn by Benedict Cumberbatch left me in pieces; Dan Gilroy's *Night Crawler* (2014) felt like a bleakly funny fever dream. The nights were long, my sleep interrupted by Spanish nurses taking bloods and checking my readings. The days were battles with leg-bags and the cumbersome tap that released my piss. Every time it seemed I might go home my temperature spiked and my hopes were dashed. When I finally got there, film proved too much for me and I succumbed to the narcotic pleasures of long-form TV.

Propped up in the sitting room watching Danish procedural *The Killing* (2007) I began to get some insight into why film was dying and TV thriving. The bait and switch of long-form narrative, endlessly edging towards revelations then snatching them away, and the richly populated narrative foreground kept me marooned in essentially the same place for twenty hours – well, I had time to fill and TV is masterly at killing time. Twenty hours – that's ten films! The very idea of watching ten films is too exhausting to contemplate when you're depleted; all that intensity, all that work to enter new narratives again and again, all those choices to make: ten versus one. No, better to stay put and linger in one endless story which artfully diverts but moves inexorably further from its source reality.

I crawled back to work at the UEA in Norwich, where I was now running an MA in Scriptwriting. At the end of a long seminar my catheter broke loose, dousing me in urine and I ran to the loos batting away puzzled students. But worse than this was the news that mum, who'd been experiencing chronic symptoms whose cause had eluded her doctors, had been rushed into hospital in extreme pain. Dad, terrified, called me from Bristol. I had to go there.

Somehow, I dragged my leaky body down to see her, limping round Paddington, camped near the train loo. Ironically it was dad we'd feared for, after a decade-long struggle with prostate cancer, the very gland now bedevilling me. Pale and hairless from his chemo, his neck swollen, he picked me up from Temple Meads and drove to a new-build hospital in Southmead. We navigated this cathedral of a place to find her ward; I was shocked at what I saw.

Mum, still in her early 70s, lay in a deep morphine torpor, face lined with pain. She was able to sit up and drink tea from a child's beaker; she let me brush her hair, walk her gently into the sit-down shower. On her bedside table were unopened new books and a diary with only one entry: *'I'm worried about Derek.'*

The noises from the doctors were grave; she had a form of leukaemia, diagnosed so late that the endless transfusions in her broken veins were achieving little. Two days later, with supreme irony Mother's Day, she was vanishing in front of us. At noon a young head-scarfed doctor cradled mum, leaning in to gain assent to end the treatment prolonging her pain. Sue joined us from Surrey. In that darkening room the three of us sat, moistening mum's lips, watching her grow lighter as her breath grew more pained; by ten, a nurse from the Philippines informed us it would not be long before she was *'with God'*. We held her as her life went – it honestly felt like that.

The velocity of mum's death left us blindsided; but now the challenge was to support dad, bereft of his partner of almost sixty years. Every aspect of his life was symbiotically interwoven with hers. In their small house in Ham Green, they were at the epicentre of a network of friends despite waning health. Her presence was in every room: the meals frozen in the freezer labelled in spidery script, the drawers of spices in pots acquired in my childhood, jars of jam still not ready to eat, or her garden where dad and I would now have to replace her fine work with our rough approximations.

I got better, commuting as frequently as I could to Bristol. The pattern established itself; dad picked me up at the station, reparking at the docks, we'd potter over the new bridge to Canon's Marsh, browse the second-hand book stalls, lunch at the Watershed, and watch the afternoon film. This ritual continued for eighteen months as his health dwindled.

I chose the films and invariably got it wrong. Sean Foley's *Mindhorn* (2016) was a rookie error; its humour far too pastichey for him and too broad for me; Ben Wheatley's *High Rise* (2015) was an even bigger misfire, its louche Ballardian chaos chimed with me but bored him stupid (where's the bloody narrative? No heroes, even flawed ones!) He scorned sci-fi which struck him as pointlessly unreal. I thought he might enjoy Hirokazu Koreeda's wise family drama *After the Storm* (2016) but he was snoring in the first five minutes. And through his eyes I did find contemporary films well, too small, too modest, too nichey, too localised in their concerns – film's great period of adventure and risk disavowed for particular passions, auditions for TV programmes, small but not resonant stories. But on one occasion I got it absolutely right.

Hell or High Water (2016) by Scottish director David McKenzie describes itself as a western/thriller and Taylor Sheridan's dynamic script about two brothers compelled by poverty to hold up banks in rust-belt West Texas nicely revamps archetypes guaranteed to keep us both happy. British cinematographer and former nature documentarian Giles Nuttgen's images of a desiccated post-oil landscape capture the ecological fallout of the carbon economy, the scrub ablaze as cowboys salvage their herd, and into the blackened chaos come cougars and coyote, ghosts of a lost landscape. As we follow the brothers back to their homestead we realise one of them (Toby) has nursed his mother into an early grave, and when the other, Tanner, announces, '*We're like the Comanches, brother, Lords of the plain*', the lineage to the great American western is clearly established. Add in the parallel plot of an ageing Jeff Bridges as Texas Ranger Marcus Hamilton slyly advancing on the felons, and the deal is sealed; hearing his rallying cry, '*I have one hunt left in me*', I could see dad's smile flash in the dark.

This was a happy 90 minutes, grief set by and pain forgotten, even if he was in the loo as quick as I could get him when the lights came up. Watching it and watching him watching it I was taken right back to how this had all began; the unseen *Soldier Blue*, the shared pleasure of *The Outlaw Josey Wales*, the continuous conversation we'd had about films as ways into an ethics of the world, the role of violence, the elusiveness of justice. For all the script leaned too much into the unexamined gender and racial backwash of the genre, this was a very new, very sharp film, with flashes of action – ah, action, and dad's predilection for what mum called '*action-packed*' films – and bringing forensic attention to tough working-class lives. I'd hit the jackpot!

And the film did speak to the year we were advancing into. Dad, who'd used his retirement to get an Open University degree in History, and who harboured an almost unhealthy passion for Tony Blair, had been canvassing door to door in the Brexit referendum for Remain, in a Leave constituency presided over by Liam Fox, an MP he despised. The ensuing victory for Brexit felt like a personal blow to him. He'd spend his fading energies arguing against his Tory-voting retired buddies who kindly indulged him. Now '*this idiot*' Trump was on the horizon. McKenzie's film tellingly dramatised the bitter passions and frustrations that would unite abandoned American communities (as Marcus says, '*All these little towns. Dying*') with blighted '*left-behind*' British ones – let alone those in Hungary, Russia, Turkey – to vote in bullying populist throwbacks. Bridges' Marcus is a habitual racist with his underwritten partner Parker, who's part Native American part Hispanic. The bank robbers intimidate tellers of uncertain migration status, while Marcus dubs one bank manager as, '*an expert on foreclosure*'. Yes, the film tours the ruins of the world that dad had once thrived in. Afterwards we turned over this new reality, the lost optimism of his youth, the heyday of social democracy, I could only nod at his sense of loss in sad agreement. And as for Jeremy Corbyn's tenure of his party – well, my play *Limehouse* attempted to examine what happens when Labour tacks to the left as the world turns right.

In weekdays I was on campus at UEA engaged in overdue debates about decolonisation, cultural appropriation and trans rights, but watching the world beyond us succumb to regression just when we needed progressive solidarity as never before. In my teaching I placed the writing of films and plays on a pedestal, while turning my attention to the form displacing both of them, on-demand long-form television. As director after director (Baumbach, Cuaron, the Coen brothers, Scorsese) took the Netflix coin, giving up on the struggle to get a theatrical release, and writers relished their new role turning out hour after hour of what was generally known as '*content*', film's pre-eminence began to look fragile. Yet ironically - and belatedly – women directors were redefining the medium, whether the cryptic work of Argentinian director Lucrezia Martel, whose anti-colonial fable *Zama* (2017) called out the diminishing scope of her peers, or Valeska Grisebach's *Western* (2017), puncturing sentimental images of European unity with its subtle indictment of German eco-capitalism in Bulgaria. Film, never more necessary in its radical reach, was threatened by TV's irrepressible supply of comfort food.

In Norwich I'd doggedly spend my nights in Cinema City where three screens occupy a medieval merchant's house faced with flint. The programming was conservative; live-streamed theatre and galleries, middle-brow comedy pitched at older viewers and watched by them. Yet in East Anglia as a whole film-making was resurgent, with Andrea Arnold's seminal *Fish Tank* (2009) turning the working-class world of Essex's marshes into cinema gold or Joanna Hogg shooting her dazzling memoir of the early 80s, *The Souvenir* (2019), in Norfolk, or, or Guy Myhill's *The Goob* (2014) documenting the arable badlands near King's Lynn, or Andrew Haigh transposing David Constantine's tale of a marital sundering, '*Another Country*', to the flatlands of the Broads in *45 Years* (2015). Films, great films, were still being made, *are* still being made! – but only after increasingly protracted processes and with less and less impact.

Europe too seemed in retreat; I'd had a ringside seat, working with three fellow playwrights from Poland, Croatia and Germany to fashion a chaotic report from a continent reeling from the Eurozone crisis, *Europa* (2013). We were in Dresden one snowy February as neo-Nazis descended on the city to mark the anniversary of the British firebombing in 1944. I stood with fellow theatre-makers creating a human ring round the old town to keep them at bay. In 2015 the catastrophe of the endless Syrian conflict led to a migration crisis polarising the continent and in the week before the Brexit vote I travelled to Calais to document those supporting the so-called Jungle camp there, writing *The Play About Calais*. Europe's crisis even brought opportunities; I was commissioned to write a comedy about the civil servants delivering their impossible Brexit brief; would this be my TV breakthrough? Everyone in the production company seemed to love it. Maybe Europe's loss would be my gain.

And everyone who was anyone was working in television. Whereas in the past that would involve an apprenticeship on a returning soap, now with platforms proliferating worldwide, a gold rush was on and the gods governing our imagination were released from obligation to nation or audience: Netflix, Amazon, Sky, all seemed bottomless in their munificence. Who could resist the allure of the long-form? Why settle for 90 minutes when you can have ten hours? Why limit yourself to one audience when the entire world awaits you? The notion of work being '*dropped*' all at once, of audiences '*bingeing*' on it in one sitting surely empowered the dramatist as never before.

I can't tell you how many times I've slid about on sofas in Farringdon or Soho seeking my bit of the bonanza, rushing home intoxicated, hammering out my one-pager, lucky enough to be paid to knock it into a full treatment, and then, bingo, maybe advance to full script. People I respect turn it over, knock it about, pitch it back to me, kick it up to the commissioners. Confidence runs high, we hold our breath. Then, well, very little eventuates.

A typical meeting takes place in a huge Art Deco hotel in the secluded Mayfair, a part of London so wealthy even the air comes with a price tag. A genial American, fresh in from LA, having seen *Limehouse*, wants to meet me. I arrive early and he's receiving some other supplicant, unsmiling and inscrutable as they run through their '*ideas*'. I sit discreetly at one remove but can't help hearing my hapless counterpart stammering through their pitch. It seems to be set in the future, they usually are, possibly 2050, yeah, why not. *It's a world where* . . . (now it goes quiet) . . . *and there's this new kind of tech where* . . . (now a waiter takes my order) . . . *then, in series two, we really get to the* . . . (I check my watch, sip my mint tea) . . . *and we have interest from* . . . I drift into the expensive hush of the loo where crisp linen towels sit smugly in a wicker basket and ambergris-like soap softly seems to dispense itself. I look at myself in the wall-length mirrors – can I bring myself to believe in this? Why not? Haven't films, dramas, plays always started this way, in places like this? What makes me any better than that waffling dude out there? To be honest my ideas are probably even less concrete and valid than his. I breathe in and try not to look too middle-aged, too dusty, too bookish.

Dad somehow lasted into 2018. I was delighted he managed to see *Limehouse* in 2017 which took the pulse of the Labour Party he loved by examining the fate of the party he left it for, the SDP. But by Christmas that year he'd declined fast; my sister and me kept up a relay race of visits to his world which was shrinking daily. A brand-new hospital bed was installed in his living room. I sat with him into the night watching films he barely lifted his head to see but which provided him with that flicker of comfort, of the on-going life that drama – film - offers. We watched *Child 44* (2015) again and again, dad's delight at Tom Hardy's laboured Rooshan accent unfeigned, Hardy embodying the kind of masculine danger he'd always craved. There were so many films between us now, so many attempts on his Netflix account to settle on something he loved, often to no avail.

Despite carers coming at intervals, despite wheelchairs and ready meals, despite the visits of friends and upping of meds, he was moved to a hospice on the top floor of a former chocolate factory in Keynsham. Sitting there among the dying, tended to with great kindness, he moved between morphine-induced hallucinations and moments of great clarity, smiling at a vision of a dog in his room, fulsomely praising his nurses, reeling off improvised plans to solve the housing crisis. Then he'd simply eat ice cream and demand I turn off the news. Dad, asking me to turn off the news!

To kill time, I drove his car to nearby Compton Dando on the River Chew, walked into its secret clefts and vales, listening out for an early woodpecker, had a cry. Returning to the car, I took a call. It was the likeable head of the production company who'd worked with me for a year on my sure-fire TV comedy about Brexit; how was I doing? Not great, I said. I poured out my situation; he sighed, kindly – well, he'd got bad news – the sure-fire comic hit about Brexit had been killed off by the new head of Channel 4. Sorry.

I realised I felt nothing but relief. The thing was full of lame humour and thin characters. I blushed with shame in the cold dark. Back at the hospice as a piece of idle chat I told dad the news; he seethed despite his discomfort. But why be angry at something so impersonal, so random? How much did TV really matter to me anyway? Its industrial imperative to last as long as is possible, its need to sit in the domestic space and be shaped to it, whatever its edgy claims – it became clear to me all at once television is the opposite of film and theatre and I'd waste no more time on it.

Some nights I'd drive back in mum's car to Ham Green and fill the silence with film: Baumbach's sublime *The Meyerowitz Stories* (2017) provoking pained laughter in its hospital sequences; Olivier Assayas's eerie *Personal Shopper* (2016). The empty house full of his clothes and her things, their photographs, their artefacts, felt like the set dressing for their lives and the film yet to be made of them. It would make a beautiful film in some ways; their childhood caught in the manner of a Powell and Pressburger film, say, *I Know Where I'm Going* (1945) which cheered my mother-in-law through her last months, its enchanted wartime Hebrides reminding her of her courtship with her lost husband. God, Powell and Pressburger, suddenly I wanted to see all their films again: yes, *A Canterbury Tale* (1944), or *Black Narcissus* (1947), or *The Life and Times of Colonel Blimp* (1943).

No, maybe not Powell and Pressburger, maybe it should be more like Bill Douglas in his trilogy; no, too harsh in tone – more like a Terence Davies film, say, *Distant Voices, Still Lives* (1988), yes, exactly like that. God, I'd love to see that again. And their courtship would be a Karel Reisz movie or even, yes, of course something by Lindsay Anderson. As to their relocation to the Midlands that would require, well, a Ken Loach for sure, himself a Coventry lad, anything from *Up the Junction* (1968) onwards; and their final location in Bristol – more difficult. Haneke's *Amour* (2012) captures the pain and struggle of it but there'd need to be humour; well, perhaps Alan Bennett but only if Alan Bennett were to be directed by Yasujiro Ozu. But then would that be a film they watched or a film they were in? And would that be the same film I was in, my sister was in, my friends were in?

As he moved into his last phase, Sue and I camped out in his room listening to his fight for breath, waves beating the shore, his massive body unwilling to go. We were there at the end, holding his huge waxy hands. The passion of this, the nurses on hand, attendant, the whole love of the hospice turned to us, watching life pass, watching his frame battle the advance of disease into the core of breath itself – I won't cheapen it with some cross-reference, some allusion. But it had grandeur to it, a vitality that only religious art or great poetry or great film can capture.

Later we drove back to the house once more, drilled through the phone book and broke the news to friends and family, to people we knew and didn't know. We drank gin, feasted on remnants and out of sheer elation we went to the theatre – the Bristol Old Vic – to see Andrew Bovell's fine play *These Things I Know to Be True* (2016); and we went home and slept in the beds of our parents like orphans.

The next day we walked to the River Avon through woodlands and spring's stirrings; the mudbanks were primeval and ribbed and the herons spaced like musical staves on the far shore. And I could imagine, yes, a tracking shot as long and as steady as imaginable taking this all in, redeeming it in some way, as Bazin or Kracauer might have it, its deep focus like the gaze of a god, putting us all in the picture.

Epilogue: *Bande de Filles* – Coming Attractions?

Lockdown.

Suddenly a peripatetic life reduced to one street, a daily walk, a weekly clap for health workers and long days in the house. A longed-for revival of *The Contingency Plan* is cancelled on the first day; the directors heroically rehearse the cast on Zoom, and I stare at the actors marooned in tiles in their various spare rooms and sense the theatre and the world turning dark. The diary is a daily reminder of cancelled shows, engagements, seminars, journeys. Idiotic populist leaders strut, fret and gaslight; the poor suffer and die the most, in favelas, in red-lined districts, or, shockingly, in the very hospitals they clean. George Floyd is murdered by a cop in Minneapolis.

In relative comfort I am housebound with my family. Every night we gravitate to the television and try to get interested in the signature dramas, retreating into old sit-coms or streamed Shakespeare. The idly promised twelve weeks of lockdown expands into four months; then '*post-normality*' begins, in some ways a more confusing place of new protocols, masked faces, mixed messages. The new Bond movie release is endlessly kicked down the road – cinemas falter open and then shut again in the absence of any major release.

We dub Saturday night movie night. It becomes, as it has always been, a kind of ritual. I drink my weekly beer, we scroll, regretfully, through Amazon. And there awaits a fragment of lost time: *Smiles of a Summer Night* (1955), Bergman's only funny film, laced with our shared love of Sweden and flashes of theatre; *Les Enfants du Paradis* (1945), Marcel Carne's finest work, served by one of the greatest screenplays of all time by Jacques Prevert, and the dazzling performances of Jean-Louis Barrault and Maria Casares – oh, and she's also in Cocteau's dazzling dream of a film *Orphée* (1950), well, that's for next week. Films about theatre, films about performance, films about magic, films about the lives we have lost.

The long weeks taper to the excitement of Saturday night and the darkened cave of black-and-white films flickering in our living room. But while film serves as a consolation, if it remains that it'll be finally done with. The pastness of film, the hours and hours of greatness that have become more accessible than ever before, serve as a standing reproach to the timid present. But to mean anything, film needs a future as well as a past.

And here I learn from my children; Miriam in particular insists on my seeing the work of Céline Sciamma, a director on my radar but not in my purview. *Portrait of a*

Lady on Fire (2019) I admire for its silences, its painterly postbox framings, its *grisaille* shots of the Brittany coast and the intensity of its central trio of performances. But somehow it feels a little too tasteful, a little too thin in focus, a little too backward in its glance. But then we watch her previous film *Girlhood – Bande de Filles* (2014).

There is an established tradition of French films that attempt to take the measure of the so-called *banlieues*, those benighted projects of exclusion on the outskirts of Paris which warehouse people of colour, migrants, those of non-European heritage as Jonny Pitts's *Afropean* (2019) so brilliantly describes. First out the gate was *La Haine* by Matthieu Kassovitz in 1995, a riposte to the curdling nostalgia latent in French film; then came *The Class* (2008) by Laurent Cantet, a dissection of an inner-city school breaking under the weight of the project of *laïcité* , described by critic Peter Bradshaw as like a '*glass of cold water*'. Then there's Jacques Audiard's uncanny and ambivalent *A Prophet* (2009) revealing the prison system as a tinderbox of racial tension and launching the career of Tahar Rahim of Algerian heritage, who also graces the only French film by Asghar Farhadi, *The Past* (2013); Audiard then delivered his own account of the *banlieues* in *Dheepan* (2015). Yet for all the potency of these films they barely begin to confront anything but masculine experience.

Into that absence comes *Girlhood*.

Karidja Touré, its heroine Mariam, was discovered by Sciamma in an amusement park; and while the film can be, and has been, critiqued as a white middle-class French woman's projection onto its young black performers, there's no doubt the film belongs to Touré. She commands every shot and we watch in Crystel Fournier's steadycam gaze her character metamorphosise from obedience to the crackling male aggression that controls her *cité*, embodied in her brutal brother, to become 'Vic', a street-fighting, Rihanna-singing, sex-positive author of her own destiny; then, finally, with breasts bound and hair shaved, she moves invisible in and out of the Parisian boho world to which she delivers drugs. As in the equally momentous *Moonlight*, Sciamma breaks this coming of age into statuesque episodes marking Mariam's epiphanies, tracked alone in a skyscape of concrete, distant Paris obscured by La Défense, her throbbing inner life caught in the waves of Para One's electro-symphonic score.

We sat in our dark comfortable enclave at the end of the film shattered and moved – and, yes, educated and changed. It's one thing to invoke the future of film as female, something so overdue it's almost comic, it's another to note the explosion of talent of directors, writers and actors of colour, or to nod to Sciamma's inversion of the '*male gaze*' into her own notion of a film made out of '*units of desire*' – and queer desire at that. But film, for so long a platform for white male desire is being reinvented with every stroke of this key and the films that ensure its future are being made by an increasingly diverse community: Alice Rohrwacher, Chloe Zhao, Maren Ade, Mati Diop, Amma Asante, Debra Granik to name but a few.

For to submit to a film is to enter into a world and a world view all at once; to have the modesty to step out of the light and to gaze at another. In the wrong hands this process is objectification and voyeurism; but under the aegis of a director and writer as gifted as Sciamma, armed with exquisite tact and an eye for the poetics of the form, everything formulaic is removed and the character looks us in the eye, enters our world as much we enter theirs.

Our fractured and damaged world is too often run by narcissists who see only themselves wherever they look; the power of film, and theatre, offers nothing less than a true way of being in the world. For all my middle-aged pessimism I believe that call is ultimately irresistible.

And as I write this Trump has been voted out and a coronavirus vaccine has arrived. Soon enough we will return, masked and hushed, into our cinemas and theatres, away from the comfort blanket of the online and the small screen and back into the drama of life. And the great films awaiting us will show us the world anew and help us live in it afresh.

Select Filmography and Bibliography

Preface: *Dark Waters* – The Last Movie?

FILMS

All the President's Men (1976), (FILM), Dir. Alan J. Pakula, USA: Wildwood Enterprises
Carol (2015), (FILM), Dir. Todd Haynes, USA: Number 9 Films
Dark Waters (2019), (FILM), Dir. Todd Haynes, USA: Participant
Don't Look Now (1973), (FILM), Dir. Nicolas Roeg, UK: Casey Productions
Far from Heaven (2002), (FILM), Dir. Todd Haynes, USA: Consolidated Film Industries
Klute (1971), (FILM), Dir. Alan J. Pakula, USA: Gus Productions
The Parallax View (1974), (FILM), Dir. Alan J. Pakula, USA: Paramount Pictures
You Can Count on Me (2000), (FILM), Dir. Kenneth Lonergan: Paramount Classics

BOOKS

Bazin, André, 'Tout film est un documentaire social' in Les Lettres françaises, 166 (July 1947)
Cavell, Stanley (1980), *The World Viewed: Reflections on the Ontology of Film,* Cambridge MA: Harvard University Press
Hobsbawm, Eric (1994), *The Age of Extremes: The Short Twentieth Century, 1914–1991,* London: Little, Brown
Kracauer, Siegfried (1960), *Theory of Film: The Redemption of Reality,* London: Oxford University Press

1. *The Wizard of Oz*: Primal Screen (Coventry)

FILMS

Bad Company (1972), (FILM), Dir. Robert Benton, USA: Paramount Pictures
Cars (2006), (FILM), Dir. John Lasseter, USA: Walt Disney Pictures
The Culpepper Cattle Co. (1972), (FILM), Dir. Dick Richards, USA: Twentieth Century Fox
The Graduate (1967), (FILM), Dir. Mike Nichols. USA: Mike Nichols/Lawrence Turman Productions
Hangmen Also Die (1943), (FILM), Dir. Fritz Lang, USA: Arnold Pressburger Films
Les Quatre Cents Coups (1959), (FILM), Dir. Francois Truffaut, France: Les Filmes du Carosse
Little Big Man (1970), (FILM), Dir. Arthur Penn, USA: Cinema Center Films

Salome, Where She Danced (1945), (FILM), Dir. Charles Lamont, USA: Walter Wanger
   Productions
Scrooge (1970), (FILM), Dir. Ronald Neame, UK: Cinema Center Productions
Soldier Blue (1970), (FILM), Dir. Ralph Nelson, USA: Katzka-Loeb
Summer with Monika (1953), (FILM), Dir. Ingmar Bergman, Sweden: Allan Ekelund
The Silent Village (1943), (FILM), Dir. Humphrey Jennings, UK: Crown Film Unit
This Gun for Hire (1942), (FILM), Dir. Frank Tuttle, USA: Paramount Productions
The Wizard of Oz (1939), (FILM), Dir. Victor Fleming, USA: Metro-Goldwyn-Mayer

BOOKS

Benjamin, Walter (1997), *Charles Baudelaire: A Lyric Poet in the Era of High Capitalism,*
   London: Verso
Brown, Dee (1970), *Bury my Heart at Wounded Knee,* New York: Holt, Rinehart and Winston
James, Henry (1974), *In the Cage, and Other Stories,* London: Penguin Modern Classics
Larkin, Philip (1964), 'The Large Cool Store' in *The Whitsun Weddings,* London: Faber &
   Faber
Sontag, Susan (2002), 'Fascinating Fascism' in *Under the Sign of Saturn: Essays,* London:
   Picador

2. *Logan's Run*: Deep England (Long Lawford)

FILMS

Carry on Dick (1974), (FILM), Dir. Gerald Thomas, UK: The Rank Organisation
Chinatown (1974), (FILM), Dir. Roman Polanski, USA: Penthouse
Dirty Harry (1971), (FILM), Dir. Don Siegel, USA: The Malpaso Company
The Exorcist (1973), (FILM), Dir. William Friedkin, USA: Hoya Productions
Jaws (1975), (FILM), Dir. Steven Spielberg, USA: Richard D. Zanuck
Kes (1969), (FILM), Dir. Ken Loach, UK: Woodfall Film Productions
Lawrence of Arabia (1962), (FILM), Dir. David Lean, UK: Horizon Pictures
Logan's Run (1976), (FILM), Dir. Michael Anderson, USA: Metro-Goldwyn-Mayer
The Omen (1976), (FILM), Dir. Richard Donner, USA/UK: Mace Neufeld Productions
Planet of the Apes (1968), (FILM), Dir. Franklin J. Schaffner, USA: APJAC Productions
The Railway Children (1970), (FILM), Dir. Jason Figgis, UK: Elstree Productions
La Règle du Jeu (1939), (FILM), Dir. Jean Renoir, France: Nouvelle Édition Française
Rollerball (1975), (FILM), Dir. Norman Jewison, USA: United Artists
THX 1138 (1971), (FILM) Dir. George Lucas, USA: American Zoetrope
The Towering Inferno (1974), (FILM), Dir. Irwin Allen, USA: Twentieth Century Fox
The Vampire Lovers (1970), (FILM), Dir. Roy Ward Baker, UK: Hammer Film Productions
Walkabout (1971), (FILM), Dir. Nicolas Roeg, UK: Max L. Raab-Si Litvinoff Films
Zardoz (1974), (FILM), Dir. John Boorman, UK: John Boorman Productions Ltd.

BOOKS

Clare, John (2000), 'The Gypsy Camp' in *Selected Poems,* London: Penguin Classics

Nolan, William F. (1970), *Logan's Run*, London: Corgi
Shoard, Marion (1980), *The Theft of the Countryside,* London: Maurice Temple Smith

3. *Nosferatu the Vampyre*: Into the Art House (Rugby)

FILMS

A Clockwork Orange (1971), (FILM), Dir. Stanley Kubrick, UK: Polaris Productions
Alien (1979), (FILM), Dir. Ridley Scott, USA: Twentieth Century Fox
The American Friend (1977), (FILM), Dir. Wim Wenders, West Germany: Filmproduktion
American Graffiti (1973), (FILM), Dir. George Lucas, USA: Lucasfilm
Bad Timing (1980), (FILM), Dir. Nicolas Roeg, UK: Recorded Picture Company
Carrie (1976), (FILM), Dir. Brian de Palma, USA: Red Bank Films
Closely Observed Trains (1966), (FILM), Dir. Jiri Menzil, Czechoslovakia: Barrandov Studios
Downfall (2004), (FILM), Dir. Olivier Hirschbiegel, Germany: Constantin Film
Emmanuelle (1974), (FILM), Dir. Just Jaeckin, France: Trinacra Films
Five Easy Pieces (1970), (FILM), Dir. Bob Rafelson, USA: BBS Productions
If . . . (1968), (FILM), Dir. Lindsay Anderson, UK: Memorial Enterprises
The Lost Honour of Katharina Blum (1975), (FILM), Dir. Volker Schlondorff and Margaretha
    von Trotta, West Germany: Bioskop Films
Mad Max (1979), (FILM), Dir. George Miller, Australia: Kennedy Miller Productions
The Man Who Fell to Earth (1976), (FILM), Dir. Nicolas Roeg, UK: British Lion Films
Nosferatu the Vampyre (1979), (FILM), Dir. Werner Herzog, West Germany: Werner Herzog
    Productions
O Lucky Man! (1973), (FILM), Dir. Lindsay Anderson, UK: Warner Bros.
The Outlaw Josey Wales (1976), (FILM), Dir. Clint Eastwood, USA: The Malpaso Company
Performance (1970), (FILM), Dir. Nicolas Roeg and Donald Cammell, UK: Goodtimes
    Enterprises
Raging Bull (1980), (FILM), Dir. Martin Scorsese, USA: United Artists
One Plus One (Sympathy for the Devil) (1968), (FILM), Dir. Jean-Luc Godard, UK: Cupid
    Productions
2001: A Space Odyssey (1968), (FILM), Dir. Stanley Kubrick, UK: Stanley Kubrick Productions
Taxi Driver (1976), (FILM), Dir. Martin Scorsese, USA: Columbia Pictures
The Shining (1980), (FILM), Dir. Stanley Kubrick, USA: The Producer Circle Films
This Sporting Life (1963), (FILM), Dir. Lindsay Anderson, UK: A Julian Wintle Leslie Parkyn
    Production
Der Himmel über Berlin (Wings of Desire) (1987), (FILM), Dir. Wim Wenders, West Germany:
    Road Movies Filmproduktion

BOOKS

Bazin, André, (2005) 'Theatre and Cinema' in *What is Cinema? Vol 1.*, essays selected and
    translated by Hugh Gray, Berkeley: University of California Press
Bennett, Alan (2004), *The History Boys*, London: Faber & Faber
Herzog, Werner (2019), *Scenarios 111*, Minneapolis: University of Minnesota Press
Hughes, Thomas, (2008) *Tom Brown's Schooldays*, Oxford: Oxford World Classics

4. *Solaris*: Learning to Dream (Dunchurch)

FILMS

Andrei Rublev (1966), (FILM), Dr. Andrey Tarkovsky, USSR: Mosfilm
Apocalypse Now! (1979), (FILM), Dir. Francis Ford Coppola, USA: Omni Zoetrope
Archipelago (2010), (FILM), Dir. Joanna Hogg, UK: Wild Horses Film Company
Bicycle Thieves (1948), (FILM), Dir. Vittorio de Sica, Italy: Produzioni di Sica
Breaking Away (1979), (FILM), Dir. Richard Yates, USA: Twentieth Century Fox
The Bridge on the River Kwai (1957), (FILM), Dir. David Lean, UK: Horizon Pictures
Dark Star (1974), (FILM), Dir. John Carpenter, USA: Jack H. Harris Enterprises
Fanny and Alexander (1982), (FILM), Dir. Ingmar Bergman, Sweden: Gaumont
Hearts of Darkness: A Filmmaker's Apocalypse (1991), (FILM), Dir. Eleanor Coppola,
    Zoetrope
Lacombe Lucien (1974), (FILM), Dir. Louis Malle, France: Nouvelles Éditions
    de Films
Merry Christmas, Mr Lawrence (1983), Dir. Nagisa Oshima, Japan: Recorded Pictures
    Company
Mirror (1975), (FILM), Dir. Andrey Tarkovsky, USSR: Mosfilm
Les Mistons (1957), (FILM), Dir. Francois Truffaut, France: Les Films du Carrosse
Silent Running (1972), (FILM), Dir. Douglas Trumbull, USA: Universal Pictures
Solaris (1972), (FILM), Dir. Andrey Tarkovsky, USSR: Mosfilm
Stalker (1979), (FILM), Dir. Andrey Tarkovsky, USSR: Mosfilm

TELEVISION

Abigail's Party (1977), (TV Programme), BBC 2, November 1977
Brideshead Revisited (1981), (TV Programme), ITV, October 1981
Pennies from Heaven (1976), (TV Programme), BBC 1, March 1978

BOOKS

Barker, Howard (1985), *A Passion in Six Days,* London: Calder Publications
Beckett, Andy (2015), *Promised You a Miracle: Why 1980–1982 Made Modern Britain,*
    London: Allen Lane
Dyer, Geoff (2013), *Zona: A Book about a Film about a Journey to a Room,* Edinburgh:
    Canongate
Leavis, F. R. (1948) *The Great Tradition,* London: Chatto & Windus
Park, James (1984), *Learning to Dream: New British Cinema,* London: Faber & Faber
Reynolds, Simon (2005), *Rip It Up and Start Again: Postpunk 1978–1984,* London: Faber &
    Faber
Tarkovsky, Andrey (1986), *Sculpting in Time,* London: Bodley Head
Thomson, David (1994), *A Biographical Dictionary of Film,* London: André Deutsch
Truffaut, Francois (1978), *Hitchcock,* London: Granada Publishing
Waters, Steve (2017), *Limehouse,* London: Nick Hern Books
Willis, Paul (1977), *Learning to Labour,* Farnborough: Saxon House

5. *Shoah*: Living Dangerously (Israel)

FILMS

The Deerhunter (1978), (FILM), Dir. Michael Cimino, USA: EMI
Die Falschung (Circle of Deceit) (1981), Dir. Volker Schlondorff, Germany: Kino International
The Killing Fields (1984), (FILM), Dir. Roland Joffe, UK: Goldcrest Films
Nuit et Brouillard (Night and Fog) (1956), (FILM), Dir. Alain Resnais, France: Argos Films
One from the Heart (1981), (FILM), Dir. Francis Ford Coppola, USA: Zoetrope
Parasite (2019), (FILM), Dir. Boon Jong-Ho, South Korea: Barunson E&A
Satantango (1994), (FILM), Dir. Bela Tarr, Hungary: Vega Film
Schindler's List (1993), (FILM), Dir. Steven Spielberg, USA: Amblin Entertainment
Shoah (1985), (FILM), Dir. Claude Lanzmann, France: New Yorker Films
Sophie's Choice (1982), (FILM), Dir. Alan J. Pakula, USA: ITC Entertainment
Swimming to Cambodia (1987), (FILM), Dir. Jonathan Demme, USA: The Swimming Company
The Year of Living Dangerously (1982), (FILM), Dir. Peter Weir, Australia: Metro-Goldwyn-Mayer
Waltz with Bashir (2008), (FILM), Dir. Ari Folman, Israel: Bridgit Folman Film Gang

TELEVISION

The Jewel in the Crown, (TV Programme), Granada TV, January 1981

BOOKS

Conrad, Joseph (2007), *Lord Jim*, London: Penguin Classics
Conrad, Joseph (2007), *Nostromo,* London: Penguin Classics
Foden, Giles (1998), *The Last King of Scotland,* London: Faber & Faber
Greene, Graham (2004), *The Honorary Consul,* London: Penguin Classics
Greene, Graham (2002), *Journey without Maps*, London: Vintage Classics
Kember, Paul (2015), *Not Quite Jerusalem,* London: Samuel French
Waters, Steve (2003), *World Music*, London: Nick Hern Books

6. *Vagabond*: Male Gazes (Oxford)

FILMS

Ali: Fear Eats the Soul (Angst essen Seele auf) (1974), (FILM), Dir. Rainer Werner Fassbinder, West Germany: Tango-Film
Á Nos Amours (To Our Loves) (1983), (FILM), Dir. Maurice Pialat, France: Artificial Eye
A Zed and Two Noughts (1985), (FILM), Dir. Peter Greenaway, UK: Channel 4 Films
Betty Blue (1986), (FILM), Dir. Jean-Jacques Beineix, France: Gaumont
Blade Runner (1982), (FILM), Dir. Ridley Scott, USA: The Ladd Company
Blue Velvet (1986), (FILM), Dir. David Lynch, USA: De Laurentiis Entertainment Group
Caravaggio (1986), (FILM), Dir. Derek Jarman, UK: Zeitgeist Films
Diva (1981), (FILM), Dir. Jean-Jacques Beineix, France: Les Films Galaxie

Drowning by Numbers (1988), (FILM), Dir. Peter Greenaway, UK: Prestige

Edward II (1991), (FILM), Dir. Derek Jarman, UK: BBC Films

Effi Briest (1974), (FILM), Dir. Rainer Werner Fassbinder, West Germany: Tango Film

The Marriage of Maria Braun (1978), (FILM), Dir. Rainer Werner Fassbinder, Germany:
   Albatros Filmproduktion

Eraserhead (1977), (FILM), Dir. David Lynch, USA: AFI Center for Advanced Studies

Fox and His Friends (Faustrecht der Freiheit) (1975), dir. Rainer Werner Fassbinder,
   Germany: Tango Film

The Hit (1984), (FILM), Dir. Stephen Frears, UK: Recorded Picture Company

Inland Empire (2006), (FILM), Dir. David Lynch, USA: Absurda

Last Tango in Paris (1972), (FILM), Dir. Bernardo Bertolucci, Italy: Produzioni Europee
   Associati (PEA)

Paris Nous Appartient (Paris Belongs to Us) (1961), (FILM), Dir. Jacques Rivette, France:
   Les Films du Carosse

Partie de Campagne (1936), (FILM), Dir. Jean Renoir, France: Joseph Burstyn Inc

Querelle (1982), (FILM), Dir. Rainer Werner Fassbinder, Germany: Gaumont S.A. Paris

Privileged (1982), (FILM), Dir. Michael Hoffman, UK: Oxford University Film Foundation

Repo Man (1984), (FILM), Dir. Alex Cox, USA: Edge City Productions

The Social Network (2010), (FILM), Dir. David Fincher, USA: Columbia Pictures

The Tempest (1979), (FILM), Dir. Derek Jarman, UK: Boyd's Company

The Wicker Man (1973), (FILM), Dir. Robin Hardy, UK: British Lion Films

Theorem (1968), (FILM), Dir. Pier Paolo Pasolini, Italy: Aeotos Produzioni Cinematografiche

Vagabond (San Toit, Ni Loit) (1985), Dir. Agnes Varda, France: MK2 Diffusion

Veronika Voss (1982), (FILM), Dir. Rainer Werner Fassbinder, Germany: Rialto Films

WR: Mysteries of the Organism (1971), Dir. Dusan Makavejev, Yugoslavia: Neoplanta Film

BOOKS

Deleuze, Gilles and Guattari, Felix (1983), *The Anti-Oedipus: Capitalism and Schizophrenia,*
   Minneapolis: University of Minnesota

Derrida, Jacques (1984), *Signesponge/Signsponge,* New York: Columbia University Press

Eagleton, Terry (2008), *Literary Theory: An Introduction,* Oxford: Wiley-Blackwell

Foucault, Michel (1990), *The History of Sexuality: Vol. 1,* London: Vintage

Genet, Jean (2015), *The Balcony (Le Balcon),* London: Faber & Faber

Hughes, Robert (2006), *Culture of Complaint: The Fraying of America,* Oxford: Oxford
   University Press

Jameson, Frederic (1971), *Marxism and Form,* Princeton: Princeton University Press

Mulvey Laura (2009), *Visual and Other Pleasures,* London: Palgrave Macmillan

Swift, Jonathan (2008), *'A Tale of a Tub' and Other Works,* Oxford: Oxford University Press

7. *Comrades*: Working-Class Heroes (Bristol)

FILMS

Alice in den Stadten (Alice in the Cities) (1974), (FILM), Dir. Wim Wenders, West Germany:
   Axiom Films

A Private Function (1984), (FILM), Dir. Malcolm Mowbray, UK: Handmade Films

Auto-da-fe (2016), (FILM), Dir. John Akomfrah, UK: Smoking Dogs Films

Comrades (1986), (FILM), Dir. Bill Douglas, UK: Film 4 Productions

Le Gai Savoir (1969), (FILM), Dir. Jean-Luc Godard, France: ORTF

Handsworth Sounds (1986), (FILM), Dir. John Akomfrah, UK: Black Audio Film Collective

Im Lauf der Zeit (Kings of the Road) (1976), (FILM) Dir. Wim Wenders, West Germany: Axiom Films

Le Mépris (1963), (FILM), Dir. Jean-Luc Godard, France/Italy: Rome-Paris Films

Looking for Langston (1989), (FILM), Dir. Isaac Julien, UK: BFI

My Beautiful Laundrette (1985), (FILM), Dir. Stephen Frears, UK: Working Title Films

My Ain Folk (1973), (FILM), Dir. Bill Douglas, UK: BFI

My Childhood (1972), (FILM), Dir. Bill Douglas, UK: BFI

My Way Home (1978), (FILM), Dir. Bill Douglas, UK: BFI

Nashville (1975), (FILM), Dir. Robert Altman, USA: ABC Motion Pictures

Numero Deux (1975), (FILM), Dir: Jean-Luc Godard, France: Sonimage

Le Petit Soldat (1960/3), (FILM), Dir. Jean-Luc Godard, France: Société Nouvelle du Cinéma

Pierrot le Fou (1965) (FILM), Dir. Jean-Luc Godard, France: Rome-Paris Films

Radio On (1979), (FILM), Dir. Chris Petit, UK: British Film Institute

Tout Va Bien (1972), (FILM), Dir. Jean-Luc Godard, France: Anouchka Films

Tropikos (2016), (FILM), Dir. John Akomfrah, UK: Arts Council

Vivre Sa Vie (1962), (FILM), Dir. Jean-Luc Godard, France: Films de la Pléiade

Winstanley (1975), (FILM), Dirs. Kevin Brownlow, Andrew Mollo, UK: BFI

Young Soul Rebels (1991), (FILM), Dir. Isaac Julien. UK: BFI

TELEVISION

Shoestring, (TV Programme), BBC 1, September 1979

BOOKS

Adorno, Theodor (2005), *Minima Moralia: Reflections from a Damaged Life,* London: Verso

Debord, Guy (1984), *Society of the Spectacle,* Kalamazoo: Black & Red

Ehrenreich, Barbara (2009), *Smile or Die*, London: Granta

MacCabe, Colin (1983), *Godard: Images, Sounds, Politics,* London: BFI Productions

Samuel, Raphael (1996), *Theatres of Memory*, London: Verso

Waters, Steve (2009), *The Contingency Plan*, London: Nick Hern Books

Williams, Raymond (1989), 'Culture is Ordinary' in *Resources of Hope*, London: Verso

Wright, Patrick (1985), *On Living in an Old Country: The National Past in Contemporary Britain*, London: Verso

8. *The White Hell of Pitz Palu*: Date Movies (Oxford)

FILMS

Alphaville (1965), (FILM), Dir. Jean-Luc Godard, France: Chaumiane

Die Angst des Tormanns beim Elfmeter (The Goalie's Anxiety at the Penalty Kick) (1972), (FILM), Dir. Wim Wenders, West Germany: Bauer International
Dead Poet's Society (1989), (FILM), Dir. Peter Weir, USA: Touchstone Pictures
Diner (1982), (FILM), Dir. Barry Levinson, USA: Metro-Goldwyn-Mayer
Ghostbusters (1984), (FILM), Dir. Ivan Reitman, USA: Columbia Pictures
Goodfellas (1990), (FILM), Dir. Martin Scorsese, USA: Warner Bros
The Hustler (1961), (FILM), Dir. Robert Rossen, USA: Rossen Enterprises
McCabe and Mrs Miller (1971), (FILM), Dir. Robert Altman, USA: Warner Brothers
The Virgin Spring (1960), (FILM), Dir. Ingmar Bergman, Sweden: Janus Films
Die Weisse Hölle von Piz Palü (The White Hell of Pitz Palu) (1929), (FILM), Germany: H. R. Sokal-Film GmbH

BOOKS

Berkoff, Steven (1988), *The Trial, Metamorphosis, In the Penal Colony: Three Theatre Adaptations from Franz Kafka,* London: Amber Press
Butor, Michel (1960), *Degrees*, London: Methuen
Buchner, Georg (1979), *Woyzeck*, London: Methuen
Chalmers, Hero (2004), *Royalist Women Writers, 1650–1689*, Oxford: Oxford University Press
Daly, Macdonald (1999), *A Primer in Marxist Aesthetics,* London: Zoilus
Handke, Peter (1971), *Offending the Audience/Self Accusation,* London: Methuen
Marshall, James Vance (1959), *Walkabout (The Children)* New York: Doubleday and Co.

9. *Reservoir Dogs*: Screen Play (Birmingham)

FILMS

El Angel Exterminador (The Exterminating Angel) (1962), Dir. Luis. Bunuel, Mexico: Barcino Films
Le Charm Discret de la Bourgeoisie (The Discreet Charm of the Bourgeoisie) (1972), (FILM), Dir. Luis Bunuel, France: Greenwich Film Productions
House of Games (1997), (FILM), Dir. David Mamet, USA: Filmhaus
Inglourious Basterds (2009), (FILM), Dir. Quentin Tarantino, USA: A Band Apart
Glengarry Glen Ross (1992), (FILM), Dir. James Foley, USA: Zupnik Enterprises
Homicide (1991), (FILM), Dir. David Mamet, USA: Triumph Films
Insignificance (1985), (FILM), Dir. Nicolas Roeg, UK: Recorded Picture
Jackie Brown (1997), (FILM), Dir. Quentin Tarantino, USA: Miramax
Once Upon a Time in Hollywood (2019), (FILM), Dir. Quentin Tarantino, USA: Columbia Pictures
Persona (1966), (FILM) Dir. Ingmar Bergman, Sweden: AB Svensk Filmindustri
Pulp Fiction (1994), (FILM) Dir. Quentin Tarantino, USA: Miramax
Reds (1981), (FILM), Dir Warren Beatty, USA: Barclays Mercantile Industrial Finance
Reservoir Dogs (1992), (FILM), Dir. Quentin Tarantino, USA: Miramax
Things Change (1998), (FILM), Dir. David Mamet, USA: Columbia Pictures
Wetherby (1985), (FILM), Dir. David Hare, UK: Film 4 International

TELEVISION

Country (1981), (TV Programme), BBC One, October 1981

BOOKS

Brecht, Bertolt (1948) *The Caucasian Chalk Circle* trans. James and Tanya Stern, London: Methuen

Edgar, David (1997) *Edgar: Plays: One: The Jail Diary of Albie Sachs, Mary Barnes, Saigon Rose, O Fair Jerusalem, Destiny*, London: Methuen

Edgar, David (1990), *Edgar Plays: Two: Ecclesiastes, The Life and Adventures of Nicholas Nickleby Pts 1 and 2, Entertaining Strangers*, London: Methuen

Edgar, David (1990) *The Shape of the Table*, London: Nick Hern Books

Fuegi, John (1994), *The Life and Lies of Bertolt Brecht,* London: Harper Collins

Griffiths, Trevor, (2007) *Theatre Plays One* (including *The Party* and *The Cherry Orchard*), London: Spokesman Books

Hare, David (1996) *Plays One: Slag, Teeth 'n' Smiles, Knuckle, Licking Hitler, Plenty*, London: Faber & Faber

Johnson, Terry (1993) *Plays One: Insignificance, Unsuitable for Adults, Cries from the Animal House* London: Methuen

Kane, Sarah (2001) *Complete Plays: Blasted, Phaedra's Love, Cleansed, Crave, 4.48 Psychosis, Skin*, London: Methuen

McIntyre, Clare (1994), *My Heart's a Suitcase* and *Low Level Panic*, London: Nick Hern Books

Mamet, David (1992) *Oleanna*, London: Methuen

10. *Winter Light*: Marriage Story (Cambridge)

FILMS

Alfie (1966), (FILM), Dir. Lewis Gilbert, UK: Paramount

Au Hasard Balthazar (1966), (FILM), Dir. Robert Bresson, France: Cinema Ventures

Un Condemné à Mort est Échappé (*A Man Escaped*) (1956), (FILM), Dir. Robert Bresson, France: Gaumont

Four Weddings and a Funeral, (1994), (FILM) Dir. Mike Newell, UK: Polygram Filmed Entertainment

Georgy Girl (1966), (FILM), Dir. Silvio Narazzano, UK: Everglades Productions

Germania, Anno Zero (*Germany Year Zero*) (1947), (FILM), Dir. Roberto Rossellini, Italy/West Germany: Produzione Salvo D'Angelo

Jeanne La Pucelle (Joan the Maid) Pts 1 and 2 (1994), (FILM), Dir. Jacques Rivette, France: France 3 Cinema

Lancelot du Lac (1974), (FILM), Dir. Robert Bresson, France: Mara Films

Mouchette (1966), (FILM), Dir. Robert Bresson, France: UGC/CFDC

Notting Hill (1999), (FILM), Dir. Roger Michel, UK: Polygram Filmed Entertainment

Paisan (1946), (FILM), Dir. Roberto Rossellini, Italy: Organizzazione Film Internazionali

La Passion de Jeanne d'Arc (*The Passion of Joan of Arc*) (1928), (FILM), Dir. Carl Dreyer, France: Societe Generale des Films

Pretty Woman (1990), (FILM), Dir Garry Marshall, USA: Touchstone Pictures

Procès de Jeanne d'Arc (*The Trial of Joan of Arc*) (1962), (FILM), Dir. Robert Bresson, France: Agnes Delahaie Productions

The Rider (2017), (FILM), Dir. Chloe Zao, USA: Caviar Highwayman Films

Sense and Sensibility (1995), (FILM), Dir. Ang Lee, UK: Columbia Pictures

Shallow Grave (1994), (FILM), Dir. Danny Boyle, UK: Channel 4 Films

The Silence (1963), (FILM), Dir. Ingmar Bergman, Sweden: Svensk Filmindustri

The Searchers (1956), (FILM), Dir. John Ford, USA: C. V. Whitney Pictures

Through a Glass Darkly (1961), (FILM), Dir. Ingmar Bergman, Sweden: Svensk Filmindustri

Trainspotting (1996), (FILM), Dir. Danny Boyle, UK: Channel 4 Films

Winter Light (1963), (FILM), Dir. Ingmar Bergman, Sweden: Svensk Filmindustri

BOOKS

Behn, Aphra (1999), *The Rover*, London: Nick Hern Books

Bergman, Ingmar, '*The Making of Film*', Filmnyheter 19-20, December 1954, pp. 1–9.

Brecht, Bertolt, (1982), *Happy End: A Melodrama with Songs*, London: Samuel French

Bresson, Robert, (2017), *Notes on the Cinematograph*, New York: The New York Review of Books

Cartwright, Jim (1990), *Road*, London: Methuen Modern Classics

Durrenmatt, Friedrich (1962), *The Visit (Der Besuch der Alten Dame)*, trans. Patrick Bowles, London: Jonathan Cape

Friel, Brian (1995), *Translations,* London: Faber & Faber

Ibsen, Henrik (1964), *Hedda Gabler and Other Plays*, trans. Una Ellis-Fernor, London: Penguin

Ravenhill, Mark (1996), *Shopping and Fucking*, London: Methuen

Stein, Joseph (1964), *Fiddler on the Roof,* London: International Music Productions

Synge, John Millicent (2008), *The Playboy of the Western World and Other Plays,* Oxford: Oxford University Press

Vogler, Christopher (1992), *The Writer's Journey: Mythic Structure for Storytellers,* Studio City CA: Michael Wiese Productions

Waters, Steve (2015), *Temple*, London: Nick Hern Books

Wertenbaker, Timberlake (2015), *Our Country's Good*, London: Methuen

11. *Code Unknown*: Cosmopolis (London)

FILMS

Amour (2012), (FILM), Dir. Michael Haneke, France: Les Films du Losange

Benny's Video (1992), (FILM), Dir. Michael Haneke, Austria: Bernard Lang

Blow-Up (1966), (FILM), Dir. Michelangelo Antonioni, Italy/UK: Premier Productions

Caché (Hidden) (2005), (FILM), Dir. Michael Haneke, France: Les Films du Losange

Code Inconnu (Code Unknown) (2000), (FILM), Dir. Michael Haneke, France: Arte France Cinéma

Crash (2004), (FILM), Dir. Paul Haggis, USA: Bob Yari Productions

Ladybird, Ladybird (1994), (FILM) Dir. Ken Loach, UK: Channel 4 Films

Lantana (2001), (FILM), Dir. Ray Lawrence, Australia: Australian Film Finance Corporation
London (1994), (FILM), Dir. Patrick Keiller, UK: BFI Production
The Long Goodbye (1973), (FILM), Dir. Robert Altman, USA: E-K-Corporation
The Low Down (2001), (FILM), Dir. Jamie Thraves, UK: Bozie
Magnolia (1999), (FILM), Dir. Paul Thomas Anderson, USA: Ghoulardi Film Company
Nil by Mouth (1997), (FILM), Dir. Gary Oldman, UK: EuropaCorp
The Passenger (1975), (FILM), Dir. Michelangelo Antonioni, Italy/France/Spain: Metro-Goldwyn-Mayer
Rancid Aluminium (2000), (FILM), Dir. Edward Thomas, UK: Ballpark Productions Partnership
Second Coming (2004), (FILM), Dir. debbie tucker green, UK: BFI
71 Fragments of a Chronology of Chance (1994), (FILM), Dir. Michael Haneke, Austria: ARTE
Short Cuts (1993), (FILM), Dir. Robert Altman, USA: Fine Line Features
The White Ribbon (2009), (FILM), Dir. Michael Haneke, Germany: X-Filme Creative Pool
Wonderland (1998), (FILM), Dir. Michael Winterbottom, UK: BBC

BOOKS

Bovell, Andrew (2009), *Speaking in Tongues*, London: Nick Hern Books
Hare, David (1998), *The Blue Room,* London: Faber & Faber
Marber, Patrick (1997), *Closer*, London: Methuen
Schnitzler, Arthur (2014), *La Ronde*, London: CreateSpace Independent Classics
Sinclair, Iain (1997), *Lights Out for the Territory*, London: Granta
Waters, Steve (2002), *After the Gods*, London: Faber & Faber
Waters, Steve (2011), *Little Platoons,* London: Nick Hern Books
Wenders, Wim (1986), *Emotion Pictures,* London: Faber & Faber
Wilson, Lanford (2002) *Burn This*, London: Joseph Weinberger Plays

12. *The Wind Will Carry Us*: Life during Wartime (Cambridge, Cairo, Kyiv, Greeley, Sheffield, Leeds)

FILMS

A Diary for Timothy (1946), (FILM), Dir. Humphrey Jennings, UK: Crown Film Unit
The Apartment (1960), (FILM), Dir. Billy Wilder, USA: The Mirisch Company
The Apple (1998), (FILM), Dir. Samira Makhmalbaf, Iran: Makhmalbaf Productions
Battle for Haditha (2007), (FILM), Dir. Nick Broomfield, UK: Channel 4 Films
Blackboards (2000), (FILM), Dir. Samira Makhmalbaf, Iran: Makhmalbaf Productions
Close Up (1990), (FILM), Dir. Abbas Kiarostami, Iran: Kanoon
Les Cousins (1959), (FILM), Dir. Claude Chabrol, France: Les Films Marceau
Fahrenheit 9/11 (2004), (FILM), Dir. Michael Moore, USA: Dog Eat Dog Films
Four Lions (2010), (FILM), Dir. Chris Morris, UK: Film 4 Productions
The Hurt Locker (2008), (FILM), Dir. Kathryn Bigelow, USA: Voltage Pictures
In This World (2002), (FILM), Dir. Michael Winterbottom, UK: The Film Consortium
Kandahar (2001), (FILM), Dir. Mohsen Makhmalbaf, Iran: Makhmalbaf Productions

Once Upon a Time in Anatolia (2011), Dir. Nuri Bilge Ceylan, Turkey: Zeyno Film

La Quattro Volte (2010), (FILM), Dir. Michelangelo Frammartino, Italy: Invisible Film

The Quince Tree Sun (1992), (FILM), Dir. Victor Erice, Spain: Euskal Media

The Road to Guantanamo (2006), (FILM), Dir. Michael Winterbottom, UK: Film 4 Productions

A Separation (2010), (FILM), Dir. Asghar Farhadi, Iran: Asghar Farhadi Productions

Taste of Cherry (1997), (FILM), Dir. Abbas Kiarostami, Iran: Abbas Kiarostami Productions

Tehran Taxi (2015), (FILM), Dir. Jafar Panahi, Iran: Jafar Panahi Film Productions

Thomas and the Magic Railroad (2000), (FILM), Dir. Britt Alcroft, UK: Gullane Pictures

A Time for Drunken Horses (2000), (FILM), Dir. Bahman Ghobad, Iran: Bahman Ghobadi Films

Time Code (2000), (FILM), Dir. Mike Figgis, UK: Screen Gems

The Time That Remains (2008), (FILM), Dir. Elia Suleiman, Palestine: The Film

Twelve Years a Slave (2013), (FILM), Dir. Steve McQueen, USA: New Regency Productions

Up (2009), (FILM), Dir. Pete Docter, USA: Walt Disney Pictures

Uzak (Distance) (2002), (FILM), Dir. Nuri Ceylan Bilge, Turkey: NBC Productions

Wadjda (2012), (FILM), Dir. Haifaa al-Mansour, Saudi Arabia: Razor Film Produktion GmbH

Wall-E (2008), (FILM), Dir. Andrew Stanton, USA: Walt Disney Studios

The Wild Pear Tree (2018), (FILM), Dir. Nuri Bilge Ceylan, Turkey: NBC Film

The Wind Will Carry Us (1999), (FILM), Dir. Abbas Kiarostami, Iran: Abbas Kiarostami Productions

Winter Sleep (2014), (FILM), Dir. Nuri Bilge Ceylan, Turkey: NBC Film

Zero Dark Thirty (2012), (FILM), Dir. Kathryn Bigelow: Columbia Pictures

TELEVISION

Britz, (TV Programme), Dir. Peter Kosminsky, Channel 4, October 2007

The Government Inspector, (TV Programme), Dir. Peter Kosminsky, Channel 4, March 2005

BOOKS

Burke, Jason (2012), *The 9/11 Wars*, London: Penguin

Brittain, Victoria, and Slovo, Gillian, (2004), *Guantanamo*, London: Oberon

Carr, Matthew (2010), *The Infernal Machine*, London: C. Hurst and Co. Publishers

Carr, Matthew (2012), *Fortress Europe*, New York: New Press

Kaufman, Moises (2000), *The Laramie Project*, London: Vintage

Smith, Anna Deavere (1992), *Fires in the Mirror*, New York: Dramatists Play Service

Smith, Anna Deavere (1994), *Twilight: Los Angeles 1992*, New York: Dramatists Play Service

Waters, Steve (2008) *Fast Labour*, London: Nick Hern Books

Waters, Steve (2012) *Ignorance/Jahiliyyah*, London: Nick Hern Books

Waters, Steve (2013) *Europa*, London: Bloomsbury

13. *An Inconvenient Truth*: Green Screens (Impington)

FILMS

Age of Stupid (2009), (FILM), Dir. Franny Armstrong, UK: Spanner Films
An Inconvenient Truth (2006), (FILM), Dir. Davis Guggenheim, USA: Laurence Bender
  Productions
The Day After Tomorrow (2004), (FILM), Dir. Roland Emmerich, USA: Twentieth Century Fox
Days of Heaven (1978), (FILM) Dir. Terrence Malick, USA: Paramount Pictures
Encounters at the End of the World (2007), (FILM), Dir. Werner Herzog, USA: Discovery
  Films
Grizzly Man (2005), (FILM), Dir. Werner Herzog, USA: Lions Gate Films
Home (2009), (FILM), Dir. Yann Arthus-Bertrand, France: Europacor
The Killer Inside Me (2010), (FILM), Dir. Michael Winterbottom, UK: Hero Entertainment
The Last King of Scotland (2006), (FILM), Dir. Kevin MacDonald, UK: Cowboy
Leave No Trace (2017), (FILM), Dir. Debra Granik, USA: BRON Studios
Meek's Cut-Off (2010), (FILM), Dir. Kelly Reichardt, USA: Evenstar Films
Moonlight (2016), (FILM), Dir. Barry Jenkins, USA: A24
My Dinner with Andre (1981), (FILM), Dir. Louis Malle, USA: Saga Productions Inc
Night Moves (2013), (FILM), Dir. Kelly Reichardt, USA: Maybach Film Productions
The Power of Community: How Cuba Survived Peak Oil (2006),(FILM), Dir. Faith Morgan,
  USA: AlchemyHouse Productions
The Road (2009), (FILM), Dir. John Hillcoat, USA: 2929 Productions
Shame (1968), (FILM), Dir. Ingmar Bergman, Sweden: Svensk Filmindustri
Vanya on 42nd Street (1994), (FILM), Dir. Louis Malle, USA: Channel 4 Films

BOOKS

Bartlett, Mike (2010), *Earthquakes in London*, London: Methuen
Carrière, Jean-Claude (1994), *The Secret Language of Film*, London: Faber & Faber
MacMillan, Duncan (2011), *Lungs*, London, Oberon
Waters, Steve (2010), *The Secret Life of Plays*, London: Nick Hern Books

14. *Hell or High Water*: Exit Music (Bristol, Cambridge, Norwich)

FILMS

A Canterbury Tale (1944), (FILM), Dir. Michael Powell, UK: The Archers
After the Storm (2016), (FILM), Dir. Hirokazu Koreeda, Japan: Aoi Promotion
Black Narcissus (1947), (FILM), Dir. Michael Powell, UK: The Archers
Child 44 (2015), (FILM), Dir. Daniel Epsinosa, Czech/UK/USA/Russia, Summit
  Entertainment
Distant Voices, Still Lives (1988), (FILM), Dir. Terence Davies, UK: BFI
Fish Tank (2009), (FILM), Dir. Andrea Arnold, UK: BBC Films
45 Years (2015), (FILM), Dir. Andrew Haigh, UK: Film 4 Productions

The Goob (2014), (FILM), Dir. Guy Myhill, UK: BBC Films
Hell or High Water (2016), (FILM), Dir. David McKenzie, USA: CBS Films
High Rise (2015), (FILM), Dir. Ben Wheatley, UK: HanWay Films
I Know Where I'm Going (1945), (FILM), Dir. Michael Powell, UK: The Archers
The Imitation Game (2014), (FILM), Dir. Morten Tydlum, UK/USA: Black Bear Productions
The Life and Times of Colonel Blimp (FILM) (1943), Dir. Michael Powell, UK: The Archers
The Meyerowitz Stories (2017), (FILM), Dir. Noah Baumbach, USA: Netflix
Mindhorn (2016), (FILM), Dir. Sean Foley, UK: BBC Films
Night Crawler (2014), (FILM), Dir. Dan Gilroy, USA: Bold Films
Personal Shopper (2016), (FILM), Dir. Olivier Assayas, France: CG Cinema
The Souvenir Part One (2019), (FILM), Dir. Joanna Hogg, UK: BBC Films
Up the Junction (1968), (FILM), Dir. Ken Loach, UK: BHE Films
Western (2017), (FILM), Dir. Valeska Grisebach, Germany: Komplizen Film
Zama (2017), (FILM), Dir. Lucrezia Martel, Argentina/Brazil: Bananeira Films

TELEVISION

(Forbrydelsen) The Killing, (TV Programme), Denmark, DR1, January 2007

BOOKS

Bovell, Andrew (2016), *These Things I Know To Be True,* London: Nick Hern Books

Epilogue: *Bande de Filles* – Coming Attractions?

FILMS

Bandes de Filles (Girlhood) (2014), (FILM), Dir. Celine Sciamma, France: Hold Up Films
Dheepan (2015), (FILM), Dir. Jacques Audiard, France: Why Not Productions
Les Enfants du Paradis (1945), (FILM), Dir. Marcel Carne, France: Société Nouvelle Pathé Cinéma
Entre les Murs (The Class), (2008) (FILM), Dir. Laurent Cantet, France: Haut et Court
La Haine (1995), (FILM), Dir. Mathieu Kassovitz, France: Canal+
Orphée (1950), (FILM), Dir. Jean Cocteau, France: André Paulve Film
Le Passé (The Past) (2013), (FILM), Dir. Asghar Farhadi, France: Memento Films Productions
Portrait de la Jeune Fille en Feu (Portrait of a Lady on Fire) (2019), (FILM), Dir. Céline Sciamma, France: Lilies Films
A Prophet (2009), (FILM), Dir. Jacques Audiard, France: Why Not Productions
Smiles of a Summer Night (1955), (FILM), Dir. Ingmar Bergman, Sweden: Svenskindustri

BOOKS

Pitts, Jonny (2019), *Afropean: Notes from a Black Europe*, London: Penguin

Lightning Source UK Ltd.
Milton Keynes UK
UKHW020044070721
386757UK00002B/28